THE HOLY GRAIL

A. D. Winans

THE HOLY GRAIL:

CHARLES BUKOWSKI

AND THE

SECOND COMING REVOLUTION

Dustbooks
Paradise, CA

7-02 Dustbooks 15⁰⁰

The author wishes to thank Kevin Ring, Beat Scene Press, England for first publishing parts of this book in a limited edition print run of five hundred copies, which were later serialized in issues of *Chiron Review*.

Photo #2, 9, and 23 were first published by Ian Griffin, Green Bean Press in a book of mine titled *North Beach Revisited* (2000).

Photo #5, 6, 12, and 22 first appeared in Brian Morrisey's *Poesy Magazine*.

Library of Congress Cataloging-in-Publication Data

Winans, A.D.

  The Holy Grail: Charles Bukowski and the Second Coming Revolution

  1. Charles Bukowski. 2. American prose literature—history and criticism.

  3. Autobiography. 4. Authors, American—biography.

PS3552.U4.W553   2002

ISBN 0-916685-94-2 (paper)
     0-916685-95-0 (cloth)

Cover and jacket design by Todd Neal, Trollbäck & Co., New York City

Dustbooks
P.O. Box 100
Paradise, CA 95967
www.dustbooks.com

10 9 8 7 6 5 4 3 2 1
First Edition

In memory of Charles Bukowski

About the author

A. D. Winans is a San Francisco poet and writer. His poetry and prose has appeared worldwide in over 500 literary magazines and anthologies. He is the author of thirty books of poetry and prose, including *North Beach Poems* and *I Kiss The Feet Of Angels.* He edited and published *Second Coming* magazine/press from 1972 to 1989. In 1974, *Second Coming* published a special Charles Bukowski issue, which is now a collector's item. In the ensuing years, *Second Coming* published Bukowski on a regular basis, which resulted in a close friendship between the two writers that lasted for over seventeen years. The material in this book details the relationship between the two men up until the death of Bukowski in March 1994.

Acknowledgments

"Postcard For Charles Bukowski" was first published in *Stance*. "For All Those Kids Who wrote Poems For Charles Bukowski" was first published in *Caffeine*, and re-published by Free Thought Press. "Poem For the Old Man" was first published in *Beat Scene*. "Visiting Folsom Prison" was first published by *Southern Ocean Review*, New Zealand. Some of these same poems were later published as a Lummox Press chapbook.

Parts of this book were originally published by Beat Scene Press (England), under the title *of The Charles Bukowski/Second Coming Years*, in a limited edition of 500 copies.

Introduction

Charles Bukowski and I were friends for over seventeen years.

Our friendship began in 1972, when I was editing and publishing *Second Coming* magazine/press, and continued through 1989. In 1974, *Second Coming* published a "Special Charles Bukowski" issue, which resulted in the strengthening of our friendship.

In letters, telephone conversations, and in personal meetings, Bukowski and I discussed the small press world and the role the poet has played in its development and history. Bukowski spent decades writing for small magazines before he became an established literary and financial success. Today, several years after his death, his books continue to sell throughout the world.

There are people who believe you have to break bread or drink with a person on an on-going basis before you can call that person a friend. I don't subscribe to that point of view. I never met the late William Wantling, perhaps the best poet to graduate from the U.S. prison system, but we corresponded regularly until his death in 1974, and I considered him a close friend. I personally met Bukowski less than a handful of times, but he too was a friend of mine.

Friends are there when you need them, at low points in life, when they are never more important. Bukowski wrote me once: "I know you are down and out, low on coin, spiritually molested like the rest of us; little chance but to hang on by the fingernails, work a line or two down on paper, and walk down the street and breathe the air of this shit life they've put upon us and that we've put upon ourselves."

This statement says a lot about who Bukowski was. He was a man who shot straight from the hip, the same way I have tried to do my entire life; the same way I have done in this book. I believe this is what drew Bukowski and me together. There weren't any games between us. No need to wear masks. We accepted each other for what we were, warts and all.

I knew Bukowski could tear a person apart in poems and in short stories, and he often did. In the process, he frequently took unnecessary cheap shots that hurt people who considered him their friend. It was rare for Bukowski to write a poem praising another poet, as he did with the poet Jack Micheline. At the opposite end of the spectrum, Bukowski moved me enough to write several poems for him, a few of which I have included in this book. This book is not a Hail-the-Chief-I-Love-Bukowski book. There are too many of these books in print which are almost embarrassing in their hero worship.

The truth is Bukowski was not a hero. He was like the rest of us, a man possessed with both good and bad traits. As Bukowski told me at the home of Linda King, "I haven't met a saint I like yet."

Neeli Cherkovski's book *(Hank)*, written when Bukowski was still alive, was the first Bukowski biography. The book was later re-issued, with added accounts of Cherkovski's personal experiences with Bukowski. Several years after Bukowski's death, several books were published dealing with the man's mystique. Almost without exception, these books portrayed Bukowski as the Arch Angel of literature, and this is where they fail. Bukowski wasn't the personification of Jesus or the reincarnation of Satan. He was simply one of the best poets and writers of our time.

I feel it necessary to stress the word "one." Steve Richmond's book *Spinning off Bukowski* (Sun Dog Press) leaves the reader with the false impression that Bukowski was the best writer in America. It would be difficult to prove by any standards that Bukowski was a better writer than Steinbeck or Hemingway, and equally hard to prove he was a better poet than Walt Whitman, or even Allen Ginsberg, who did more to free the language of poetry far earlier than Bukowski. What Bukowski was was the best writer to come out of the "little" magazine movement of the 60's and 70's.

One might legitimately ask why so many of Bukowski's friends and peers have tried to portray him as the Second Coming of Jesus Christ or the Jim Morrison of poetry. I guess some people have a need for a hero in their life, and in the process, confuse reality with myth. Billy the Kid and General Custer are but two examples of how history has sometimes presented two flawed men as heroes.

Bukowski was many things to many different people, but there is more to writing than whores, pimps, drunks and Sunday morning hangovers.

I don't mean to imply the books published after Bukowski's death have no useful purpose. Although the majority of the books are limited in scope, they do provide the reader with additional insight into a man who was as complex in person as his writing was direct.

The main weakness in the majority of the books that have been published on Bukowski's life is that they paint a one dimensional picture. We see Bukowski as the Robin Hood of literature. He can do no wrong. His motives and actions are in the interest of the unfortunate and the dispossessed. The truth is Bukowski betrayed and tore apart many former friends, both in short stories and in vindictive poems, frequently breaking off friendships whenever someone got too close, and often on brutal terms.

Steve Richmond, one of Bukowski's closest friends, believes the only human close to Bukowski was his daughter, Marina. The rest of us were mere characters in his personal life and work, there to be used, and so he did. For many years Bukowski and I shared a close relationship, perhaps made tighter by our infrequent one-on-one meetings. The less contact you had with Bukowski, the more he respected you, and the fewer attacks you faced. The late Marvin Malone of *Wormwood Review* is testimony to this.

It's conceivable Bukowski's inability to deal with love was largely the result of his unhappy childhood. He suffered from a skin condition resulting in disfiguring boils that left his face a road map of scars, and because of this he was often cruelly taunted by his classmates. At home, he received little or no comfort, often finding himself subjected to beatings by an ill-tempered and abusive father who, when he wasn't beating his son, took out his anger on Bukowski's mother.

If a person has never known love, it can be frightening. Love requires trust, and I don't think Bukowski trusted many people. There are numerous examples of his turning against former friends. Ann Menebroker is but one. Menebroker, a Sacramento poet, began corresponding with Bukowski in the early 60's. The two exchanged letters for several years, until Bukowski wrote and asked her to return his correspondence, after he found a buyer for his letters. Menebroker happily complied with Bukowski's request. Years later he paid her back by writing an offensive poem about her that not only was demeaning in nature, but untrue. There was no reason for the attack, but Bukowski never needed a reason. Bukowski would later turn on me as well. I wrote a poem "Small Press Poet Makes It Big," which appeared in a small midwest literary magazine. The poem was critical of Bukowski's post-fame behavior, but was written in a humorous vein and didn't mention him by name. But those who knew Bukowski knew he was the character in the poem.

Bukowski became furious, overlooking the fact that on two separate occasions he had committed acts toward me that would have caused a lesser person to break off friendship with him. But there may have been other reasons. Perhaps we had grown too close over the years and it was my turn to walk the plank. I do know life is too short for holding grudges. Rifts are all too common between writers in the literary world. Writers are a sensitive lot. It has been my experience that there exists a degree of jealousy between writers who have been published and writers who have not.

This same pettiness frequently exists between poets who have established a literary reputation and poets who haven't had the same good fortune, with recognized writers jealously guarding their turf against intrusion. Whatever the situation, I liked Bukowski too much to write him off. I valued our friendship built up over the years. So I decided to write a book about our friendship and the role he played in the *Second Coming* publishing years. The truth is Bukowski was an important part of *Second Coming*. He represented what the magazine was all about, and it could be argued he was *Second Coming*. That's the plain and simple truth.

I have never met a poet and writer who possessed Bukowski's talent. To be sure, there were many bad poems and short stories that should never have seen print, but what writer among us can truthfully say he or she hasn't suffered the same fate? No one moved me as deeply as Bukowski or had the ability to bring tears to my eyes as Bukowski did in his "Poem For Jane," and he had few rivals when it came to humor.

Bukowski's first book, *Post Office*, was written in nineteen days. The book is filled with laughter that shines through the pain of working at a dead-end job that kills a man's spirit and physically breaks him down. I know! I worked for the San Francisco post office for over five years, some of the same years that Bukowski was employed at the Los Angeles post office.

Bukowski's publisher, Black Sparrow, continues to release new Bukowski books, including past correspondence with fellow poets, writers, and small press publishers, assuring Bukowski's legion of fans that he will be with us for years to come.

Poem For The Old Man

I tried to picture him
battling leukemia
but still managing just
20 days before his death
to send a poem
to *Wormwood Review*
filled with life
right up to the end
perhaps a wry smile
on his face
for the doctor
and a hand on the ass
of the nurse
playing out the game
to the end
like only the
old man was capable
of doing

One

March 1994. I was sitting in my apartment in Noe Valley, San Francisco, reading the morning newspaper and enjoying my first morning cup of coffee. I turned to the entertainment section of the newspaper and was startled to find the obituary of Charles Bukowski. I thought it odd finding an obituary in the entertainment section of a newspaper; however, in retrospect, there was nothing odd about it at all. Bukowski had carefully scripted his reputation as a hard drinking, womanizing hero of the unfortunate and the downtrodden, the same people who bought his books and identified so strongly with him.

In the end, Bukowski became as much an entertainer as he was a poet and writer. This is evidenced by the fact that in his last years, the actor Sean Penn became one of his closest friends. I was stunned to learn Bukowski was dead at the age of seventy-three, entertainer or not.

Bukowski is on record as having said he never expected to live a long life. It's also a matter of record that in his mid-thirties, he lay near death from a bleeding ulcer in a Los Angeles hospital charity ward, the direct result of years of hard drinking and neglect of his body. I had been aware for some time that he was battling a series of ailments brought on by advanced age and abuse of his body, but had not dwelled much on the matter. Most people avoid thinking about death until it stares at them, as if not thinking about it will delay the inevitable.

In reality, death was a recurring theme in many of Bukowski's poems, especially over the last several years of his life. And it stalked Bukowski's mythical character in his final novel (*Pulp*) published shortly before his death. I was saddened we had not corresponded for several years. I don't believe this can be attributed solely to the poem I wrote about him, although it surely played a role. When I wrote the poem I didn't consider it much of a put-down, and even believed he might find it humorous, given the fact he had poked so much fun at poets and writer friends.

The truth is I might never have written the poem if Bukowski hadn't told me early in our friendship that one day I would read about his going fishing with James Dickey and Norman Mailer. He told me that when that day came I could write about it and he would understand. However, it was not Dickey or Mailer who inspired me to write the poem, as much as the presence of actor Sean Penn and other Hollywood luminaries in his life after he gained fame. Even in his wildest dreams he could never have imagined the day he would have Hollywood movie idols paying him homage; movie stars who visited his home and brought what Bukowski described as their "God-awful poems."

Putting aside my thoughts about my poem, I asked myself what role Neeli Cherkovski (formerly Cherry) might have played in the split between Bukowski and me. Neeli said of Bukowski, in a short essay appearing in a special *Second Coming* Bukowski issue, "Bukowski is a damned good man to drink with on cold winter evenings." And drink they did. Neeli had a close relationship with Bukowski in those early days before Bukowski became famous, when Bukowski lived on De Longpre Avenue in a $95 a month apartment consisting of little more than a living room, kitchen and bedroom.

Neeli was only a sixteen-year-old high school student when he first met Bukowski and had been influenced by Bukowski's book, *Longshot Poems For Broke Players*, which Bukowski dedicated to the famed jockey, Willie Shoemaker. Neeli said in his *Second Coming* essay:

"Over the years, I'd get together with Bukowski . . . He became Hank and I remained Neeli . . . Three and four day drunks, swallowing bennies like candy . . . Smoking dope, dropping acid . . . wild drives through Hollywood at two in the morning." Bukowski would call me up at three in the morning. "Hey kid, the motherfucking post office is killing me . . . I'm on the cross . . . I've got the deep blues . . . Why don't you come over for awhile?" And I'd drive over to his place and wouldn't leave for days.

I became acquainted with Neeli through North Beach readings he gave and poetry events he helped organize. I knew he was ambitious and badly wanted recognition in the local poetry circles. This made me somewhat distrustful of him. So when Bukowski told me that Neeli had told him I was saying uncomplimentary things about him (Bukowski), and only corresponded with him so I could later sell his letters, I had no reason to question Bukowski's word. It was Neeli who sold his Bukowski correspondence. The letters Bukowski wrote to me over the years are part of my archives stored at the Brown University Library. Whatever the truth is, Bukowski's comments served to strain the already fragile relationship between me and Neeli. I simply chose to quit seeing him.

Neeli and I have since patched up many of our differences, and when I later told him what Bukowski said, Neeli replied "We don't need the ghost of Charles Bukowski coming between us. Hank is a lying son-of-a-bitch if he said I put you down. He loved to see the lions fight." There is a ring of truth to what Neeli says, since it is well documented that Bukowski frequently broke off friendships with fellow poets and writers, and never needed a reason or excuse.

It has been reported that Bukowski and Doug Blazek, the former editor and publisher of *Ole*, whom Bukowski corresponded with for many years, had a strong kinship between them which ended shortly after they met in person. And John Bryan, a fringe member of the Beat generation and the former editor and publisher of *Open City*, who paid Bukowski for his column "Notes From A Dirty Old Man," is yet another small press luminary who had a falling out with Bukowski. The list is quite lengthy and includes well known small press figures like Harold Norse, Linda King, and Jon and Gypsy Lou Webb from LouJon Press. Other poets, such as Steve Richmond and Neeli Cherkovski, were also discarded by Bukowski only to be brought back later into his good graces. Yet neither of them were invited to attend Bukowski's funeral.

However, the fact remains Bukowski was hurt by the poem I wrote about him. I believe in his heart he felt I had betrayed him. He responded by writing a poem titled "Poem for the Poet up North," which was published in *Impulse*, a small Southern California literary magazine. The gist of the poem was that, because he later gained literary fame, that this somehow "gnawed" away at me. He couldn't have been more wrong.

I responded with a poem of my own ("Poem For the Poet Down South"), which was published in the same magazine. As far as I am aware, this ended the feud between us and the attacks went no further.

Bukowski went about his life doing what he did best, writing poetry and prose. I went about my life working for the Department of Education, investigating claims of discrimination while writing my own poems, prose, and essays as time permitted.

Now I found myself sitting alone in my small apartment with Bukowski on my mind. I walked over to the bookcase and removed the special Charles Bukowski issue I had published in 1974 and began thumbing through it, which brought back fond memories of those early years. When friends and fellow writers raved about Bukowski's poetry, I urged them to read his prose. I find his prose to be fast, gripping, and frequently laced with humor. In my opinion, his prose is more concise and disciplined than his poetry, which at times has a tendency to ramble on and too often reflects forced endings. This does not diminish the fact that many of his poems are as powerful as any ever written.

Taking a break and switching from coffee to beer, I remembered Bukowski's, "I Am With The Roots Of Flowers," which appeared in issue One of *The Outsider Magazine*. I believe the year was 1961. This may have been the first time I realized Bukowski's raw power as a poet. As I continued to read Hank's work throughout the day I was reminded that my own early prose writing had been influenced by F. Scott Fitzgerald and Ernest Hemingway. Bukowski confided that he found Fitzgerald's work too "polished," but readily acknowledged being influenced by Hemingway's macho style. The honesty of Bukowski's work hooked me from the beginning. If his work was not always beautiful, it was honest and moving. The same can be said for his letters. Letter writing has become a lost art (especially since e-mail), but Bukowski's letters are collector's items, bringing top dollar. And they were frequently laced with brilliance.

I became an avid Bukowski fan after reading his first novel, *Post Office*. I worked at the San Francisco Rincon Annex post office for five years until 1964. Bukowski's vivid accounts of his eleven years as a postal clerk hit home. Bukowski found it necessary to get drunk in order to survive those years, much the same as I had. But what most impressed me about the book was his ability to laugh at those painful days in a wild and beautiful way. By the time I finished the novel, I was hooked on Bukowski.

I admire the fact that in 1970, at the age of 49, he took the big gamble and resigned from the post office to become a full-time writer. It would be the turning point in his life. He took the big gamble and won. No more punching time clocks. No more having to deal with career bosses whose only purpose in life seemed to be to make other people miserable.

Hank's novel influenced me to write one of only two poems I ever wrote about my years at the post office:

Post Office Reflections

After my shift
At the post office
I'd stop for a drink
At the corner bar
And chat with Carl
The bartender
But mostly I'd just sit there
And listen to the jukebox
And there was this one old
Mail clerk who came in every
Night during his lunch break
And punched B-5
A blues song
BORN TO LOSE
And you could see the defeat
In his eyes
And I'd order another drink
And watch the wall clock
Ticking down my life
Bone ass tired from sorting
Thousands of letters
Fingers numb from stuffing
Them into pigeon holes
Black soot in my nostrils
And I smelled of sweat
And death
And kept drinking until
I felt good
Or ran out of money
Or both
And later rode
The 14 Mission bus
Home with other people
Like myself
Who stared straight ahead
Out the window

Or down at their feet
Night shift people
Like me
Who couldn't do
A nine-to-five shift
And when I got off the bus

I would walk that long walk
To my apartment
And pour myself a drink
Turn on the hi-fi
And plop my tired ass
Down on the bed
Trying to shut out
The look in the eyes
Of that old mail clerk
At the corner bar
Drinking to the music
BORN TO LOSE

Shutting out thoughts of the post office, I cut out the Bukowski obituary and tossed the newspaper aside. I walked into the kitchen and returned to the living room with a bottle of brandy. I settled back into my easy chair with a shot glass of brandy and began reading the more than eighty letters Bukowski had written me during the 70's and 80's. As I did so, I cursed myself for not keeping copies of the letters I had written him over those same years.

As I continued to drink, my mind went back to the first issue of *Second Coming* which I sent Bukowski, hoping he would submit some poems to the second issue of the magazine. *Second Coming* was dedicated to publishing all types of poetry, including writers like Doug Blazek, William Wantling, Jack Micheline, Bob Kaufman, and Bukowski. However, it was Bukowski who defined what I was trying to accomplish.

How good was *Second Coming*? *Library Journal* described it as one of the best small press magazines of its day. And Richard Morris, author and director of the now defunct Committee of Small Magazine

Editors and Publishers (COSMEP) said "The two most significant influences on contemporary west coast writing have been the Beats and Charles Bukowski. Both of them were reflected in the writing published by *Second Coming* as it became the most important San Francisco literary magazine of its era."

High praise indeed. Bukowski himself listed *Second Coming, New York Quarterly,* and the *Wormwood Review* as three of the best literary magazines for writers seriously interested in submitting their work. I would add John Bennett's *Vagabond* to that list. And like *Vagabond, Second Coming* would expand to include a book line.

When I finished reading the last of Bukowski's letters, I decided to write a book about my experiences with him, and his importance to *Second Coming.* This was a time when small presses were producing some of the best poetry being written (some of the worst too). I considered Bukowski's letters to be historically important to small press history. Bukowski's publisher, John Martin, confirmed this in a letter after I mailed him a rough draft of my Bukowski book:

"Thanks for sending this for me to read. The quotes are fine. No problems at all. It's a straightforward piece of writing and is valuable for what it says about Bukowski and the problems of small press publishing in the 1970's and 1980's."

It would take me a year to write *The Charles Bukowski/Second Coming Years*, which was published in a limited edition of 500 copies by Beat Scene Press, England. The book was never distributed in the United States, and it would take me another three years to complete the book you find in your hands.

This book is not just about my relationship with Charles Bukowski and his relationship to *Second Coming.* I have attempted to document the trials and tribulations of the small presses in the 70's and 80's, while at the same time pay tribute to the poets and writers who made *Second Coming* the success it was.

Two

Over the years I had extensive talks with Bukowski on the role of the critic in the small press. Bukowski believed that in the end the only valid criticism is a better piece of work. Bukowski and I questioned the motives of small press literary critics, having too often found ourselves in their company at parties and poetry readings. We were dismayed at the army of vultures who preferred to review the poet and his lifestyle rather than the work itself. We agreed that if a writer worked long enough, was published and gained a bit of recognition, in the end he would be unlucky enough to draw the attention of the critics.

The late Charles McCabe, a columnist for the *San Francisco Chronicle*, referred to these individuals as "time gobblers." Like McCabe, Bukowski felt if the critics couldn't attack your work, they would attack your personal life. At parties you'd notice they didn't drink, but sipped; they didn't eat, they nibbled; they didn't make love, they violated. McCabe said, "Their basic assumption seems to be that because you have become a public figure, no matter how small, they somehow have earned the right to own a piece of you." McCabe felt the worst part of all this was their intent to record your every thought and action so they might later play it back to the world, "taking delight in writing that age had destroyed your ability to write, and that you were old and burned out."

Bukowski, like McCabe, believed there was only one way to deal with this kind of critic, which was to treat them brutally. I argued that this approach would only add another enemy to a growing list. Bukowski maintained that at least it would rid you of the critic, whom McCabe had described as being "the most odious specimen on earth," and "a thief who would steal your belongings is nothing compared to the critic who would steal your soul with no remorse." Bukowski felt it was a mistake to show them the slightest bit of kindness, believing they would mistake it for weakness and go for the jugular.

As it turned out, Bukowski didn't have much reason to fear the critics. The small presses lavished praise on him while the academic world simply ignored him.

Three

I met Bukowski only a few times. The main thrust of our relationship was personal correspondence and telephone conversations. Although I was privileged over many years to have Bukowski trust me with his frequent change of telephone numbers, I made an early decision to limit personal contact with him, knowing how much he valued his privacy.

I never forced myself on him. I realized he didn't like the endless crowd of poets who frequently knocked on his door, robbing him of valuable time he felt could be spent on writing. However, the few times I met Bukowski were memorable ones, like poetry readings in the 70's (the dates have faded over the years). The first reading, sponsored by City Lights Publishing House, was at the Telegraph Hill Neighborhood Association Hall. There was a large turnout that night. Perhaps five hundred or more people had come to hear their hero read. A large number even by San Francisco standards. I can still picture the polished wooden floor and the noisy and anxious crowd waiting for Bukowski to arrive. The majority of the audience was young, with maybe a third or more of the crowd made up of older literary figures.

Many of the people in attendance were stoned on alcohol or drugs. What I remember most about that night was the stage. It was set with a simple chair, a folding table, a microphone, and a refrigerator filled with cold beer. I later learned the refrigerator filled with beer was part of Bukowski's asking price for doing the reading, and would later become a trademark of his. He milked the crowd for all it was worth before appearing from backstage to the cheering crowd. Once on stage he wasted no time in opening the refrigerator door and popping open a beer to the sound of wild cheers.

I watched him survey the crowd for several seconds before tilting back his head and drinking half of the beer. Again this simple act was met with rousing cheers. Bukowski raised his hand to quiet the crowd, a tactic that failed. Bukowski slowly took his place at the table. He began the reading with a poem filled with the kind of language the audience had come to hear. The only language Bukowski knew - street language. The kind of poems his army of fans had come to identify him with. Bukowski finished the poem to loud applause, crushing the empty beer can in one of his hammock hands and tossing it to the side of the stage. I remember thinking that no one could open a can of beer like Bukowski.

During the reading he consumed as many as twelve cans of beer. If there was anything else in the refrigerator other than beer, I couldn't make it out. In retrospect the event reminded me of the first Monterey Jazz Festival I had attended as a young man. At the time I was in awe of the musicians, just as the crowd that night was hypnotized by Bukowski. Bukowski appeared to be enjoying the attention he was receiving, but this may have partly been attributed to his drinking. I say this only because he (despite his reputation) was a shy man in those early days, especially when it came to giving public readings. It was the alcohol, and the alcohol alone, that provided him with the bravado he displayed on stage.

There were a lot of shit-and-fuck poems and some cute and clever ones. After each poem, he grinned at the audience like a leprechaun. It was an evening that left the North Beach crowd buzzing long after he left for a party hosted by Lawrence Ferlinghetti. The party was held at Ferlinghetti's apartment on upper Grant Avenue, located over the old City Lights Publishing House. Bukowski and Linda King, his lover at the time, got into a violent argument. The argument became physical, with Bukowski being pushed or falling down a flight of stairs, depending on whether you believe Bukowski's or King's version of what happened.

Either way, his face was badly scratched. During the confrontation a window was broken, and Ferlinghetti was pissed at both Bukowski and King, but any ill feelings quickly passed. I wasn't at the party when the fight broke out so I have to rely on what Linda King told Harold Norse, in a letter Norse published in his literary magazine *Bastard Angel.* To quote from her letter: "I think I would kill him [Bukowski] if he wasn't so good in bed. I didn't claw his face . . . he hit somewhere when he fell . . . I was defending my innocent self . . . I did do the biting."

Whatever the truth may be, Bukowski and Linda King had a long quarrelsome relationship. Linda said Bukowski's sensitivities were too raw and he would try to dull them with alcohol. She told Norse that their two tempers would explode "like shooting geysers," and they would "roar down an emotional roller coaster with one more fight and one more split up." The separations never lasted long. From Linda King's letter:

"After three or four hundred dollars in telephone calls, and a new woman for Bukowski and one night stands for me, we would go back to being lovers.

"It was the raw magic of sex that kept us together as long as it did. It's not because he's a great poet. He is, I know that. It's all that magic between the sheets, in the afternoon, in the morning, at midnight, the real poetry."

As for Bukowski, he said it best in a letter he wrote to the poet Jack Micheline.

"I'm really in love with this sculptress, this Linda King, man, and she writes poetry too.

"When we split, I just about go crazy. Fucking real deep down pain-agony, babe; all the coals burning, all the knifes going in, more horrible than any cancer death, that feeling, first feeling like that I've had since the death of Jane. Most women can't get to me, but this one does. She's got ways of loving, ways of being with me. Real mountain-tall magic, and most splits are my fault. I go crazy, walk out on her . . . then she leaves town or I can't find her.

"It's all too much, but I'm glad it's here, her cunt is more beautiful than the sun, and all the rest. It wasn't meant to last, but it was a wild memorable trip."

The most memorable time I spent with Bukowski was during an unexpected visit he paid me in the 70's. He wanted to visit North Beach but didn't want to drink at the bars, afraid he would run into any number of San Francisco poets he wanted to avoid. Bukowski seemed fascinated with North Beach. I took him on a tour of the old Beat bars and hangouts that had once flourished - the Coffee Gallery (now The Lost and Found Bar), the Co-Existence Bagel Shop, Mike's Pool Hall, The Place, and the San Gottardo Hotel and bar, run by an elderly French couple. I pointed out the few bars still remaining - Vesuvio's, Gino and Carlo's, Spec's, and The Saloon.

As we walked up Grant Avenue, we occasionally ran into poets and North Beach regulars I had known since the 50's and 60's. We found

Paddy O'Sullivan talking to the bartender at the Camel's Bar on the corner of Grant and Green, and stopped in to chat. Paddy was one of the more colorful characters of the Beat era, a minor poet who supported himself by hawking a pocket-sized book of his poems, *Weep Not My Child.*

You could find him almost any night of the week standing on the corner dressed in a purple cape, plumed hat, and high boots, with shoulder-length hair. He was a modern-day cavalier who greeted female tourists with a courteous bow and a kiss on the hand. Rumor has it Paddy was nothing more than a self-created myth, who followed the legendary Greenwich Village poet Maxwell Bodenheim around and stole his poems when Bodenheim died. If you asked Paddy about this, he would respond with a sly smile.

Paddy was a legend in North Beach. He would later lose his arm to a pet cheetah, but he never lost his charm. Bukowski said it was people like Paddy who gave poetry a bad name. Maybe so, I thought, but I will never forget a night at the Camel's Bar when I was stone drunk, and how Paddy saved me from a beating by a local bully. Paddy was very protective of the people he liked, and had more strength in his one arm than some people have in both. Paddy quickly subdued the bully, throwing him out into the street. When I told Bukowski this story, he said, "Well, maybe he can't write poetry, and maybe it's all a game, but he sounds like the kind of a guy I'd like to have watching my back."

I would later write a poem dedicated to Paddy O'Sullivan. I remember his coming to the reading where I first read the poem. Red-faced and proud, he embraced me and said, "You've immortalized me."

Poem For Paddy O'Sullivan

Paddy O'Sullivan
Home again wearing
The scars of the past
Like an engraved bracelet
Passed on from one lover
To another

Paddy O'Sullivan walking
The streets of North Beach
In search of old visions
Now only memories
In the nightmare of reality

Paddy O'Sullivan swapping tales
With obscene priests
Hung over with failure.

Paddy O'Sullivan of Kerouac tales
And Cassady adventures
Walking Washington Square
The bulldozer death
Lurking everywhere

Paddy O'Sullivan
Does your typewriter still
Talk to you
During the lonely hours
Of dawn?

Paddy O'Sullivan
Alone in San Francisco
Waiting on that lady poet
Who will forgive you
In the morning
For forgetting her name
In the hour of dawn
When our needs are soothed
With the power of
the written word
That stirs moves inside us
Like a runaway train
Like the haunting breath
Of a hound dog closing in
For the kill

Paddy O'Sullivan where
Have all the poets gone?
Walking straight jackets
Trapped by time.

Paddy O'Sullivan
The sun is not
As you see it now
Everything changes
And yet remains the same
The streets are no more
Or less intense
The lines on your face
Are the lines on my face
As we move back
Into the body
Into the inner self
Measured by the amnesia
Of yesterday

Paddy O'Sullivan
This town coughs up
Its dead most rudely
The raw nerve of time
Returning to haunt me
Oblivious to the thirst
Lying still at the edge
Of the river
The blueprint of life
Etched in the dark deep
Shadows of the soul

Bukowski and I walked down to Gino and Carlo's bar, owned by two Italian brothers, Aldino and Dinado. We momentarily stopped outside and exchanged pleasantries with Carl Eisenger, a sad figure of a man. Carl was a poet but hadn't written in years, after his lifetime of work was destroyed in a hotel room fire. He hadn't kept carbon copies of his poems and his life had literally gone up in flames.

Bukowski and I entered Gino and Carlo's bar, where I was warmly greeted by Dinado. On the floor in a drunken stupor lay Cheap Charley. Cheap Charley had gotten his name because he mooched free drinks at North Beach bars. Bukowski and I looked at Aldino, who was leaning over the body of Cheap Charley, pouring whiskey through a funnel down Cheap Charley's throat. The patrons cheered the action.

"Are all the poets in this area crazy?" Bukowski asked.

"Not all of them," I said.

We left the bar and headed down Grant Avenue, stopping in front of the 1232 Club, also known as the Saloon. Shoeshine Divine was standing outside clutching his custom-made shoeshine box. Shoeshine was another colorful North Beach figure who had confided to me that he was wanted by the FBI for draft evasion, which may or may not have been the truth. What made Shoeshine different was that he didn't sit on a stool but instead squatted in front of his customers, bouncing up and down like a yo-yo.

I exchanged a few barbs with Shoeshine, whom Bukowski later said had a wild look in his eyes. The kind of look that Bukowski said he had seen on the faces of men he drank with during his stone drunk days. Shoeshine left to ply his trade and Bob Seider happened to walk by, asking for spare change. Bukowski reached into his pocket and handed Seider several loose coins. Seider thanked Bukowski and left in the direction of the old Coffee Gallery. Bukowski said he didn't make it a habit to give handouts to street bums, but there was something unique in Seider's eyes. I told Bukowski that Seider had been one of the few white jazz musicians who frequented the North Beach jazz joints in the Beat days. He had played at all the small jazz clubs at the beach, charming the regulars with his smile and friendly manner. If you weren't lucky enough to catch him playing sax at the North Beach clubs, you could watch him perform free on the street near Washington Square Park. Then one day Seider pawned his sax and quit playing forever.

We walked to the Cafe Trieste, where Bukowski stopped and peered at a small group of men and women sitting at the close tables. Without warning, Bukowski said in a loud voice: "Look at all these people waiting for something to happen, only it never will." He hurried away before waiting for a response, leaving me behind to overhear a skinny woman with glasses say:

"God, did you see all that acne?" "And what a drinker's nose. He'll be dead before you know it."

The remark was met with a smattering of laughter and the young woman continued drinking her espresso. She was dead wrong! Bukowski's scars weren't from acne, but childhood boils. And he would live a relatively full life for a man who abused his body as much as he did. I managed to catch up with Bukowski a half block down the street. We didn't talk about what he said to the crowd at the Cafe Trieste. I somehow sensed this wouldn't have been the appropriate thing to do.

Bukowski was under the impression that the Beat movement began with Kerouac, Ginsberg, Cassady and the long list of Beats that the media helped make famous. There are others who would disagree. John Pyros, a writer friend, argues that the Beat movement evolved on August 6, 1945, when the first atomic bomb was dropped on Hiroshima, and ended in 1967 with the Human Be-in in San Francisco, during the last days of the Hippie Generation. Perhaps the single most important thing Kerouac, Ginsberg and Cassady did was to make rebellious young people throughout the land aware that there were others who felt the same way. I know this was the case with me.

Diane DiPrima (after reading "Howl") is quoted as having said: "I sensed he [Ginsberg] was only, could only be the vanguard of a much larger thing. All the people who, like me, had hidden and skulked . . . All these would now step forward and say their piece. Not many would hear them, but they would finally hear each other. I was about to meet my brothers."

John Pyros perhaps put it best: "To state that Kerouac and Ginsberg, et al began the Beat movement is like saying that Rosa Parks started the Civil Rights Movement . . . In fact, the land was fertile and awaited only the seed, only the spark to be kindled."

While Bukowski seemed curious about the neighborhood the Beats frequented, he did not particularly seem interested in learning the history of the Beat movement. I tried to get him to have a beer with me at Vesuvio's, located adjacent to City Lights Bookstore, which had been a favorite hangout of the Beats, but he declined. He wanted to stop by City Lights Bookstore and see Lawrence Ferlinghetti, but Ferlinghetti wasn't in.

As we continued our walk through North Beach, I clued Bukowski in on the history of City Lights Bookstore, which was founded in the 50's by Peter Martin (who later sold his interest to Ferlinghetti) and Lawrence Ferlinghetti. In the beginning, the bookstore was frequented mostly by Italian anarchists, people Martin was familiar with. (He was the son of an Italian anarchist, Carlo Tresca, who was assassinated in 1943.) Ferlinghetti also associated with the anarchist writers, many of whom were friends or acquaintances of Kenneth Rexroth, referred to by many as the "father of the Beats." City Lights began as the first all-paperback bookstore in the U.S. Even then cloth copies of books were too expensive for many working class people. It was Martin who named the store City Lights, taking the name from a Charlie Chaplin film.

On March 28, 1957, the San Francisco District Attorney's Office took City Lights to court after Allen Ginsberg's *Howl and Other Poems* (printed in England) was seized by U.S. Customs for being "obscene." The case never went to court after the U.S. district attorney declined to prosecute, forcing Customs officials to release the books. However, the San Francisco Police Department refused to ignore the matter. Ferlinghetti and Shig Muro (who at the time managed City Lights) were arrested and charged with selling "obscene literature." The American Civil Liberties Union stepped in and furnished free legal representation, hiring famed attorney Jake Ehrich to defend them.

Prominent writers and critics testified in court on behalf of City Lights, and Judge Clayton Horn set the legal precedent that if a book has the slightest redeeming social importance, it is protected under the First and Fourteenth Amendment of the U.S. and California constitutions, and therefore cannot be declared obscene. This legal precedent allowed D.H. Lawrence's *Lady Chatterley's Lover* and Henry Miller's *Tropic of Cancer* (long banned in the U.S.) to be published by Grove Press.

The San Francisco police had unwittingly put City Lights and Lawrence Ferlinghetti on the map. Not learning their lesson, the police would later return in the 60's, focusing their attention on Zap Comics and Lenore Kandal's book *Love Poems*, which only served to sell out both publications.

There are some, however, who question how courageous Ferlinghetti was in his willingness to challenge the establishment in court. Charles Plymell, a member of the 60's Beat writers, claims the battle was nothing more than challenging the right to use the word "fuck." Plymell put the matter in perspective in a lengthy interview which appeared in *Chiron Review.* Plymell challenges the establishment version of this historic event:

"Lucky that he [Ferlinghetti] probably had good coaching from his attorney brother, so he wasn't really a poor Beat poet. He knew what was happening, but why didn't he just go in the court room and say that he was Lieutenant Commander Ferlinghetti in World War Two, who had just fought for this country's freedom, and besides, this is the way sailors talk all the time. It was still close enough to WWII that the judge would have dismissed the case instantly."

Plymell compares the event to the "old downtrodden intellectual class millionaires trampled on by society," adding that the "ploy" sold a lot of books. This "thinly disguised capitalistic marketing approach" was devised by the late Allen Ginsberg, whom Plymell describes as an "ex-market researcher-cum-poet" while describing Ferlinghetti as an "ex-Navy officer-cum-bohemian-proprietor."

"P.T. Barnum couldn't have done better," says Plymell. "It was like the famous hyperbole, I saw the best minds of my generation . . . If he [Ginsberg] was looking at reality, he would have seen the best minds of his generation at Almagordo, New Mexico, playing out the old fashioned myth of power, changing the world forever."

The outspoken, straight-talking Plymell saw all this as another case of elitist capitalistic intellect at work, "screaming at the press for publicity, while building a lasting enterprise on old bohemian sympathies." It's hard to argue against Plymell. Ferlinghetti owns an expensive piece of property (City Lights Books and Publishing) in one of the most desirable locations in San Francisco, with a cabin in Big Sur and a home in Virginia, and the late Ginsberg sold his archives for over a million dollars.

Bukowski wanted to grab a bite to eat before leaving the beach, and I suggested Chinatown, which would be free of the poets Bukowski wanted to avoid. I decided to take Bukowski to Sam Wo's, a three story restaurant where you had to walk through the kitchen in order to make your way to the upstairs dining room, where the food was brought up to you on a dumbwaiter. Sam Wo's was one of the most popular "In" spots in Chinatown after the late Herb Caen, the famed San Francisco columnist, mentioned the restaurant and its waiter, Edsel

Ford, in his daily newspaper column.

As we walked through the kitchen filled with Chinese cooks wielding meat cleavers, Bukowski said, "I hope the hell you know what you're doing."

"Don't worry," I said, leading him upstairs to the dining area where we were met by Edsel Ford, the head waiter. Edsel was part entertainer, part waiter, and part madman. He told the patrons where to sit, what to order, and if you didn't like it, you were free to leave. The food was only ordinary, but the restaurant was always filled.

Edsel nodded to me in recognition as Bukowski walked beside me. Suddenly Edsel turned and shouted at Bukowski, "Single file! Single file! You stupid?" Bukowski was caught off-guard, at first growing angry and then smiling, sensing it was all part of an act. Edsel led us to a booth at the back of the restaurant and thrust a menu in our hands. I don't remember what Bukowski ordered, except that he wanted a side bowl of steamed rice. Edsel gave Bukowski a menacing look.

"No white rice. No white rice. You order fried rice," Edsel roared.

"Who ever heard of a Chinese restaurant that doesn't serve rice?" Bukowski bellowed. He finally settled on a plate of noodles, which were the best noodles in Chinatown.

After lunch I slipped Edsel a fiver and asked him to "spike" the tea. Edsel smiled and returned with an 86% proof laced pot of tea. Bukowski poured himself a drink, and said, "I think I could grow to like that guy."

We spent a considerable amount of time talking about Bukowski's favorite subject, women. I can't remember much of the conversation, but when I mentioned losing a woman I was still in love with to another man, Bukowski grew serious and said:

"You don't know what it's like to really lose a woman. When Jane died," Bukowski continued, "I knew I would never be the same. It's too painful to put down in prose. I try to put it down on paper, but it never comes out just right. I never want to bury another woman."

Bukowski talked about fame, and said becoming famous was not important to him but he would like to someday own a place of his own, even if it was only a shack. He talked about his fear of dying alone and said he hoped when his time came they would discover his body early and not find him weeks later bloated and covered with flies. Bukowski felt it was stamina that counted. He boasted that he had outlived many of the editors who had rejected his work early in the game. We talked about the small presses. Bukowski spoke highly of *Wormwood Review* and *Nola Express,* saying the latter had paid him a small sum of money for his prose pieces, and that this had helped him in his later decision to quit his job at the post office.

We talked about drugs and whether they were good for you or not. My experience with drugs was limited to grass, uppers, downers, and single experiences with peyote and LSD. Bukowski admitted to using drugs but was negative about using cocaine, which he felt was destructive. He said the only drug he was addicted to was alcohol, but found that, unlike other drugs, it didn't interfere with his writing.

I told Bukowski about my first night at North Beach when I had returned home from Panama after completing my military obligation. The first bar I visited was a beer and wine establishment called the Coffee Gallery. I was astonished at the people I saw at the bar. The women were basically dressed in black. The men wore sandals, berets, sunglasses and sported beards. It was as if they were sending out a signal they were "hip" and not part of the success-oriented general population.

Later I wandered down to the Anxious Asp, which was a jazz hangout. I was amazed by the mingling of black men and white women. Despite the liberal reputation of San Francisco, this was not something openly practiced at the time. From the Anxious Asp I made my way to the San Gottardo hotel and bar. The bar was packed that night but I managed to make my way past the crowd and ordered a beer. Before I could take a sip, I felt someone tug at my shirt from behind. I turned around and saw a woman in her thirties smiling at me.

"You want to fuck?" she said.

Before I could respond I found myself being taken by the hand and led upstairs to one of the rented hotel rooms. In short order we were naked and making love. I was only 22, and spent the next few hours locked in animal passion. Later we went downstairs for a nightcap, and heard about a party at a warehouse in the produce district. At the party we went our separate ways. The room was thick with smoke, making it uncomfortable for me. I walked into the kitchen and poured myself a drink from one of the several jugs of wine sitting on the kitchen table.

Returning to the living room, I saw a group of men and women gathered in a circle sharing a joint. In the far corner of the room a

35

young black dude was dry-humping a fat Japanese woman, whose blouse was open, exposing her ample breasts. I walked closer to the black man and his Japanese woman friend. They soon discarded their clothes and began making love with no thought to the small crowd that had gathered around to watch. Finally the black dude climbed off the woman and moved down the hall, where he disappeared into an adjacent room. I poured myself another drink and went into the room, and was startled to find the black dude and a well-built white man naked and groping each other. I felt like an uninvited voyeur and returned to the other room, where I saw the Japanese woman asleep on the floor. Shortly afterwards I too fell asleep.

When I woke up the next morning, the sun was rising and I could hear the nine-to-five people on their way to work. The Japanese woman was still asleep on the floor. I hadn't even read Jack Kerouac's *On The Road* and here I was living it.

Bukowski brought up the earlier incident at the Cafe Trieste. He said Los Angeles had its fair share of pretentious coffee houses, but he made a point to stay away from them. He described coffee houses as haunts for talentless poets and pseudo-intellectuals, whom he described as "soft boiled egg and parsley eaters."

The conversation shifted to the brawls Bukowski had gotten into as a teenager. He had been forced to defend himself because of his pock-faced looks. He lived in the slum streets of Los Angeles where survival meant being able to take care of yourself.

"Not unlike Hell's Kitchen in Chicago," he said.

In *Poetry Now*, Bukowski is quoted as saying: "The trouble is I liked it. I liked the impact of knuckles against teeth, of feeling the terrific lightning that breaks in your brain when somebody lands a clean one and you have to try to shake loose and come back and nail him before he finishes you off."

Bukowski confessed that he was too old for that kind of life anymore. We finished our spiked tea at Sam Wo's and walked to Green Street, where I had parked my car. I drove Bukowski across town to where he was staying. We awkwardly embraced, promising to stay in touch.

Four

This book is largely a memoir, and time has a way of eroding the memory. While the events described herein are factual, some of the dates may be off.

I would attend two more Bukowski readings. The one that struck me most was a reading where I had a backstage pass. I paid the $3 admission charge anyway, since I believe in paying my own way. I stood backstage near a piano and watched the old man play the audience like a violin. I later wrote a poem entitled "I Paid $3 To See Bukowski Read And Then Went Backstage And Got In For Free." The poem was published in the *New York Quarterly*. Bukowski wrote and told me that he liked the "pure honesty" of it. The poem was a virtual verbatim accounting of the reading Bukowski gave that evening and the party that followed. The kind of poem Bukowski might write himself.

The reading was a circus. Bukowski repeated his beer-drinking performance, spending much of the time verbally jousting with a small group of radical female feminists who had come to taunt him. The women never stood a chance and were quickly booed into silence by the hostile crowd, even though Bukowski defended the ladies to the audience.

The poet Jack Micheline, a longtime friend of Bukowski, was present in the audience and tried to get Bukowski to let him read a poem. But it was his show and Bukowski would have none of it. Jack had to settle for vomiting on the shoe of a minor local poet. That was the kind of night it was. At the close of the reading Bukowski thanked the audience, who whistled and yelled for an encore. Especially loud was a young man seated in the back of the auditorium who kept shouting, "More! More!" Bukowski flashed the young man an impish smile and asked how much he had paid to get into the reading. The kid took the bait.

"$3," the kid said.

"And you're a $3 audience," Bukowski shot back, much to the delight of the crowd.

Bukowski exited the building by the back of the stage, where we warmly embraced each other, getting looks from several San Francisco poets who had come to hear him read.

Bukowski asked me to ride with him to a party that was being held in his honor. I wanted nothing to do with the small band of poetry politicians and politely declined. I had parked my car a short distance from the reading and drove to the party alone. When I arrived it was wall-to-wall bodies. There were young poets who were intensely jealous of the old man mixed with the poets seeking instant fame, even though their limited talent made this next to impossible.

The old enemies were there too. I watched John Bryan edge his way close to Bukowski, whispering in a low voice, "You better watch it, my wife is here with a knife." John had told me that Bukowski had tried to put the make on his wife (Joanie) when he and Hank were still friends. I don't know if this is true or not. Bukowski would neither confirm nor deny it.

Bukowski shrugged off Bryan's remark. "Can't you forget that was in the old days?" Bukowski said. But Bryan couldn't forget because Bukowski had made it and Bryan hadn't.

There were enough poets in the room to make up a professional football team. There were poets from San Francisco and poets from Berkeley, and even one poet from New York, who was taking down notes on everything Bukowski said. It was a carnival-like atmosphere. I found my attention drawn to three women in the middle of the room. One of the women was with a male slave who was naked from the waist up, wearing a dog collar around his neck.

I was amused to see the slave had a leather leash attached to the dog collar, which his mistress held securely in one hand. The young man stood at attention, his eyes cast down at the floor. None of the women spoke to the male slave or looked him in the eye. No one else at the party paid them the slightest attention. That's the way it is in San Francisco, where people have become accustomed to the bizarre.

I watched Bukowski surrounded by men and women alike. It was as if he was a rock star and everyone wanted to reach out and touch him. The movie "Jesus Christ . . . Super Star" comes to mind, and I thought I could see a pained look on Bukowski's face.

It wasn't a night for serious conversation. It wasn't long before Bu-kowski drank himself into a semi-coma, the only way to keep sane among the crowd gathered around like hungry cannibals, feasting on his every word.

After a few beers I had to fight my way to the bathroom, only to find the room occupied in an unusual manner. The leather-clad mistress and her male slave were in the bathtub. The slave was naked and lying on his back. The woman was straddling him, forcing her slave to endure the indignity of a "golden shower."

I pretended not to look as I relieved myself. When I was through taking care of business I went into the kitchen to get myself a beer. Jack Micheline was standing next to the refrigerator surrounded by a group of admirers. Next to Bukowski, Micheline was second in demand; a silver-haired New York Bronx poet whom the poetry crowd in San Francisco had adopted as one of their own.

Micheline was talking to a young woman visiting from Australia, telling her tales of the old Beat days. When Jack spotted me he motioned for me to come over and join them. He introduced me to the young woman and left the room to discuss business with Bukowski.

I was surprised when the young woman unbuttoned her blouse, exposing two fully developed breasts with the biggest nipples I have ever seen on a woman. Without hesitation she invited me to touch them, boasting they were for real.

Within minutes we were French kissing and I felt her hand on my crotch. Suddenly she broke free from my embrace and told me that she was on antibiotics. She asked for my telephone number and said she would give me a call when she was well. I watched her leave the kitchen to talk to a young poet who was unsuccessfully trying to get Bukowski's attention.

In no time at all I had a good buzz on. I returned to the bathroom where I found Bukowski sitting on the commode with a young woman on her knees, giving him a head job. His eyes were closed but there was definitely a smile on his face. He would later write and say he didn't remember getting a blow job, but he hoped it had been a good one.

Five

The reading at the War Memorial Building in San Francisco where Bukowski read with William Stafford turned out to be a match made in hell. William Stafford, a well-known academic poet, was hardly a compatible match, given Bukowski's dislike for academic poets. I smelled disaster in the air.

I met with him before the reading, and since he was scheduled to read after Stafford, he suggested we go across the street to a bar called The Court Room. We sat at a table across from the jukebox and ordered a round of drinks. We discussed the poetry scene in San Francisco, focusing on several San Francisco poets Bukowski disliked. He seemed visibly relieved when he learned I too held these same poets in low esteem. He seemed nervous and tense and at times the conversation seemed forced.

Bukowski had the keys to Ferlinghetti's van, which was parked in an alley not far from the Veteran's Auditorium. After a few drinks we left the bar and walked to the van, where Bukowski had stashed a pint of vodka under the back seat. Bukowski sat in the back of the van while I sat in the front seat. I watched him reach under the back seat and remove a pint bottle of vodka, downing half in less than thirty seconds. I was surprised when he refused to share it with me. Perhaps sensing my hurt, he leaned toward me and said,

"A.D., I need every drop to see me through the reading. If it wasn't for the money, I wouldn't give these damn things. I'm like a beggar singing for his supper."

While sitting in the van we discussed several similarities in our lives. We had both been arrested for driving under the influence of alcohol and had spent time in the drunk tank. We both had been forced to attend traffic school and had our driver's licenses suspended. We both disliked giving poetry readings. Bukowski felt San Francisco poets were so eager for attention they begged like dogs to read at every opportunity, even at open mike readings. He said he guessed this was all right for poets just starting out, but poetry was a profession and too many poets prostituted it.

"Can you imagine a carpenter coming over to your home and working on your house for free?" Bukowski asked. He couldn't understand why a poet would get up on stage and bare his soul unless he was paid for it.

It was not hard feeling dwarfed in his presence. There was something awesome about him. His shoulders were stooped over; his hair was starting to thin; his face was a roadmap of pock marks. But his smile and wit had a way of putting you at ease.

In my correspondence with Bukowski I addressed him as Buk, as did most people he came into contact with. Bukowski said his friends called him Hank and invited me to do the same.

He and I went on to discuss other things we shared in common. Hank had gone to Los Angeles City College while I had attended City College of San Francisco. We both had unhappy childhoods, but unlike Hank's, my father had never laid a hand on me. What else did we share in common? Our sexual appetite for women, for sure. We talked about the women we had scored with and the women who had scorned us. And we shared still another thing in common - the ability to drink most people under the table.

We discussed Hank's work, which had appeared in *Outsider* and the *Los Angeles Free Press.* I told Hank how impressed I had been reading his "Notes Of A Dirty Old Man." Hank thanked me but said he didn't want to talk about the column. He nevertheless expressed his gratitude for having been paid a small sum of money for his contributions.

Another reason he hated giving poetry readings was that the organizers always expected him to attend a party afterwards. Hank said he didn't know why he attended the parties since they were almost always boring. Remembering the party Ferlinghetti had hosted and the party where I had witnessed the male slave being urinated on, I found this hard to believe.

Letting out a loud sigh, Hank finished the last of the vodka and tossed the bottle on the floor of the van. Hank said, "It's time to pay the piper," but we didn't get ten feet outside the vehicle before he turned and vomited on the side of Ferlinghetti's van. I asked him if he was okay. He told me not to worry, that it was normal for him to vomit before a reading. Hank said, "It helps steady the nerves," but I wasn't sure if he was serious or not.

Hank straightened himself up and looked perfectly sober as we walked back to the Veteran's Auditorium. I suggested we sit in the back so as not to interrupt William Stafford's reading, but he insisted on sitting closer to the front of the stage. When the crowd caught sight of Hank they began chanting "Buk, Buk, Buk." It was as if the heavyweight champion of the world was entering the ring to do battle.

Stafford paused momentarily before continuing with his reading. I felt badly for Stafford. It wasn't that I liked his poetry, which was far too academic for my taste. But he deserved more respect from Hank. Hank, on the other hand, felt no remorse at all. If anything, he seemed to enjoy the attention he was receiving from the boisterous crowd.

We sat down about eight rows from the front of the stage. Stafford concluded his reading to polite applause, quickly leaving the building. Hank pushed past the people in our row and lumbered slowly up on stage. He stood to one side as the Master of Ceremonies introduced him to thunderous applause. Flashbulbs were popping everywhere and the emotion of the audience seemed genuine.

For about forty-five minutes Hank played the audience like the master he was, smiling at the right times, tossing in jives and raw language for shock value. As usual he gave a dynamite reading. When he finished he was greeted with chants of "More, More, More." Hank read one last poem before exiting the stage, eager for another drink.

After the reading I accompanied Hank back across the street, where we resumed our earlier drinking. In between drinks we discussed the need for a writer to be alone. Hank was of the opinion that the writer is alone with his typewriter, and that everything else is a distraction. He described writer workshops as lonelyheart's clubs for writers who would never amount to anything.

"Name me one major writer who has come out of a writer's workshop?" Hank asked me. I couldn't!

I believe it was John Corrington who said, "A Bukowski poem is like the spoken voice nailed to paper." It's hard to argue with this viewpoint. How do you teach something like this at a writer's workshop? Hank wrote poetry in a language the average person could understand and identify with. Hence his popularity. Hemingway did this with prose, and then along came Bukowski to do the same with poetry.

I taught in two junior high schools where I read Bukowski's work along with other modern day poets. The kids always liked Bukowski the best. The kids also liked Jack Micheline, whom I brought into the classroom to read and discuss his poetry. I think they liked his green dyed hair too, and this was long before punk rock or Dennis Rodman came along.

Hank and I discussed the poet Harold Norse. Hank said Hal (as he referred to him) had corresponded with him while Hal was living in Paris in the 60's. Like Bukowski, Hal had also been published in *The Outsider,* I believe in the same issue featuring the work of Bukowski.

Hank said while he was forced for years to work at jobs he hated, Hal had been living the life of an expatriate. According to Hank, by the time Hal returned to the United States they had already been corresponding for several years, and when Hal returned home they became good friends.

From what I gather, while Hank was busy becoming a small press literary giant and a major voice in Europe, Hal was not getting the recognition he deserved. Hank had openly declared Hal "the best living American writer" only to have Hal grow angry over a statement Bukowski had made that no one was willing to publish Hal. Hank explained what he meant was no "major" publishing house was willing to publish Hal. He was not referring to the alternative presses, who regularly published Norse's work.

After awhile things became a bit blurred, with a never-ending number of drinks finally taking their toll on me. But I remember that Norse had a different read on what happened between him and Hank. Norse said he had been responsible for getting Hank published in the prestigious *Penguin Anthology*, and Hank had paid him back by telling his publisher (Black Sparrow) not to publish him. Both Hank and John Martin denied this.

Norse was quoted in *Bastard Angel* as saying one day Hank showed up at Norse's Venice apartment carrying a copy of *The Days Run Away Like Wild Horses,* which had just been published by Black Sparrow. Norse claims Hank said, "Hal - I was going to dedicate this book to you." But Martin said, "Why are you dedicating the book to Harold Norse? People might think you're friends." Norse said he asked Hank what he meant - were they not in fact friends? He said Hank replied, "You know me. I'm slow and didn't know what to say, so I dedicated the book to Jane, my ex-old lady."

Norse said Hank asked him not to tell John Martin about their conversation, but Norse felt the effect of the story was to drive a wedge between Norse and Martin. Norse said this incident ultimately ended their friendship, and that he left Venice to take up residence in San Francisco. Before leaving, however, he telephoned Martin and told him what had happened that day at his home in Venice. Norse said Martin was shocked but said, "You know Bukowski. He plays these games. He's only playing with you. In fact he has told me to publish you many times."

My own belief is Hank was indeed playing games with Norse as far as this incident is concerned. Hank was never a slow person, as he claimed in his conversation with Norse. The truth is you don't play games with certain people. This is especially true with someone like Norse, who is a sensitive person. Hank surely had to know that what he said to Norse was going to hurt him. Or perhaps it was one of those occasions where Hank had grown too close to Norse and was looking for an excuse to end their friendship.

Just how hurt Norse was can be found in his poem, "The Worst Thing You Can Say To Him Is I Love You," which I published in my *Second Coming* special Bukowski issue. I quote in part from the poem:

> **he does the things a real man should**
> **playing the horses**
> **winning crap games**
> **sneering at women**
> **vegetarians**
> **librarians**
> **poets**
> **sucking at 6-packs**
> **getting drunk**
> **and mean**
> **oh boy what a great writer**
> **what a smart ass clever bastard**
> **what a bleeding scarred snarling smashed**
> **GENIUS.**

Norse's poem closes by saying: "and/the worst thing you can say to him/is/I love you."

Shortly after our conversation about Norse, Lawrence Ferlinghetti came storming into the bar. I watched him angrily approach our table. I thought at first he might have discovered Hank had puked on the side of his van, but when I looked up from the table I saw he was clutching a poetry magazine which contained a poem of mine, "For Lawrence Ferlinghetti And The Old Revolution."

After exchanging greetings with Hank, Ferlinghetti "lit" into me, complaining my poem (written in response to Ferlinghetti's poem "Where Is North Beach I Can't Find It") was not true. The poem:

For Lawrence Ferlinghetti And The Old Revolution

Why must you wait for the harvest
To fail in Russia before you don
Your sailor suit again
And walk the rusted decks
Of a ghost ship that never knew
A Siberian snow field
Or saw a frozen wheat field

Why worry if the props
Won't thresh
Or there's blood in your drink
They'll never find you
Down in the boiler room
Stoking the fire

You're the Admiral of the beats
Yet missed Kerouac's wake
Because they say that
You don't like funeral

Of course nothing moves
It never does
For someone who has forgotten
How to dance in the streets.

I was not prepared for Ferlinghetti's attack, and was disturbed over the attention he was drawing from the small crowd of Bukowski admirers who had followed us to the bar.

It was while at the bar that I learned of Hank's loyalty to those he considered his friends. City Lights had just recently published a book of Hank's - *Erections, Ejaculations, Exhibitions, and General Tales of Ordinary Madness.* Hank had far more to gain by siding with Ferlinghetti than with me. If Ferlinghetti's intent was to drive a wedge between Hank and me, it failed. I'll always remember the way Hank looked up at Ferlinghetti and said, "Lawrence, that's one of the best poems I've ever read." Ferlinghetti stood for several seconds in shocked silence.

I knew my poem was an honest poem, a good poem, a poem that would be re-published many times. But I also knew it wasn't a great poem, and certainly wasn't the best poem Hank had ever read.

I watched Ferlinghetti angrily storm out of the bar and wondered how he would react when he returned to his van and found someone had puked on it.

Hank quickly finished his drink, saying he had forfeited his ride to the airport and I would need to give him a ride. As it turned out, I didn't need to take him. A young man who claimed to be a documentary filmmaker, convinced Hank to stay the night at his place, supposedly to work out the details on the proposed documentary.

I got up from the table and shook hands with Hank, leaving him with the filmmaker, and headed outside to my car. I wondered if Hank had ever read my poem for Ferlinghetti. Not that it mattered. His act of kindness is something I'll always remember.

Six

There would be one final meeting with Hank, which took place in Los Angeles at the home of Linda King. I arrived early, stopping off at several bars first. When I arrived at Linda's home, it was almost dark. I was with a Los Angeles writer who had pleaded with me to take him to meet Hank.

Hank greeted us at the front door. I immediately sensed Hank did not like RB. He had seen something about RB that I hadn't. Hank and Linda were in the company of a young man barely out of his teens. The kid sat alone in an armchair in the far corner of the room. Throughout my entire visit, I can't recall his saying a word.

Hank told me he had no idea who the kid was. The young man had shown up at the door early that morning, wanting to meet Hank. Linda and Hank had agreed to let him sleep on the couch, but Hank insisted the kid be shown the door first thing in the morning.

Throughout the evening, Hank or Linda would go into the kitchen and return with fresh drinks for RB and myself. Neither Hank nor Linda drank during my visit, which I considered odd, given their reputation. For the better part of four hours we engaged in heated literary conversation, with Hank taking on the role of devil's advocate.

It seemed that every poet I liked, Hank disliked. It wasn't until much later I learned they had remained sober in an attempt to figure me out. I found my writing dissected at great length, and at times felt uncomfortable. I didn't like being so closely scrutinized and, had I been sober, I'm sure I would have walked out. I must have passed the test. As the evening wore on, the atmosphere became more relaxed and friendly. During the entire time the kid in the corner never said a word, hardly looking our way. It was as if he was lost in a world of his own.

Hank, Linda, RB and I spent a considerable amount of time discussing Jack Micheline and his place in literature. I argued that Jack's work had been unfairly ignored, and that he was as good or better than many of the more famous Beat poets. On this count, Hank and I agreed. It became obvious that Hank liked Jack and considered him a friend. He referred to Micheline as "Brooklyn Jack, A hustling, romantic poet of the streets." But Hank also described Jack as a "screamer" who protested his fate too much.

Hank talked about Jack visiting him in Los Angeles and their drinking bouts together. Hank seemed put off that Jack would often bring along a "stack" of poems. Hank told me he didn't want to listen to the poetry of others (good or bad), but that Jack was one of the few poets who had inspired him. Hank said he occasionally wrote a poem "slamming" a poet but seldom praising, as he had done with Jack. Hank felt a lot of Jack's letters were like poems.

"How can I not like a man who enjoys going to the racetrack as much as Jack does?" Bukowski asked.

Linda occasionally broke in with a laugh, throwing her arms around Hank, saying, "He's all right. He's all right. He's no Buk, but yeah, he's all right."

The rest of the evening rapidly became a drunken blur. There were some comical stories about Neeli Cherkovski (a.k.a. Neeli Cherry). Hank recalled how Neeli would follow him around carrying a notebook, writing down every word he said, or taping their talks for future posterity. (This should be taken with a grain of salt as Hank later helped Neeli compile information for Neeli's biography of Hank). Hank mused, "When I'm dead and buried, the kid will make money off me."

Hank spoke about Neeli having a job writing speeches for a politician and walking around town with his bankbook in his pocket. "This is what money does to you," Hank said. "It's driven him mad. Absolutely mad." Hank felt Neeli had sold out, but still held out hope for him. As the evening wore on, Hank and Linda said they were retiring for the night. As I recall, Hank simply stood up and said, "It's time to call it a night." I felt like I was being dismissed from the king's court.

RB wanted to stay the night. Hank said no, but whispered to me I was free to return and sleep on the sofa, after I got rid of RB. I thanked Hank, but suffering from insomnia and finding it hard to sleep on pull-out sofa beds, I politely declined the offer.

As I prepared to head out into the night, I paused to look Hank directly in the eye. I informed him that Harold Norse had warned me that someday he (Hank) would turn against me, as he had done with Norse and others. I repeated Norse's often spoken remark that Hank couldn't stand to be loved, which drew the familiar impish smile Hank was famous for.

"And I will turn on you," Hank said.

"No, you won't," I said. My remark seemed to catch him off-guard. He wanted to know why I believed he wouldn't turn on me. "Because," I said, "what you said about the others was true. You don't know anything bad about me."

"You're right," Hank said, embracing me in a bear hug.

We shook hands and I departed for the hotel room I had rented for the night. There followed nearly two decades of personal correspondence between Hank and me, along with infrequent telephone conversations. This is the subject of the second part of this book.

Seven

In February 1958, I returned home from Panama after serving four years in the Air Force. I became interested in poetry after reading the work of Kenneth Patchen and Beat poets like Ginsberg, Ferlinghetti and Bob Kaufman. I was not then familiar with Bukowski, but became acquainted with his work shortly afterwards.

When people think of the Beat generation, they think back to the fifties: Allen Ginsberg, Jack Kerouac, and Neil Cassady. But there was a second period of creativity spanning from 1962 to 1967, and a third and longer post-Beat movement from 1967 to 1979. North Beach had a run of three decades of creativity unlike any other literary movement, and it is doubtful we will ever see another period like it.

The media likes to put labels on movements, and this was true of the 60's so-called "Hippie" movement, which flourished largely in the Haight/Ashbury district of San Francisco. When Allen Ginsberg heard what was happening on the West Coast, he left India where he had been living for years, and flew to San Francisco, where he became the self-proclaimed guru of the Hippie generation. Possessing the skills of a marketing genius, Ginsberg was a perfect fit for the Hippie movement. I was still a North Beach regular, but frequently crossed over to Haight/Ashbury, where I was raised as a child.

During this remarkable period of time, I familiarized myself with William Wantling, Doug Blazek, and Charles Bukowski. These three writers would become identified with what was known as the "Meat" school of poetry. (Poet Doug Blazek has spent over two decades trying to divorce himself from this label). It seemed almost every literary magazine contained the work of at least one of these poets. I found it mind-boggling that they seemed to share my thoughts and feelings. It was during this period that I met Bob Kaufman, the legendary black Beat poet.

I was also learning the trade of editing and publishing. I first became interested in the alternative press scene after I met veteran small press publishers like Kell Robertson (*Desperado Magazine*), Ben Hiatt

(*Grande Ronde Review*), and John Bennett (*Vagabond Magazine*), all of whom were talented poets and writers. We frequently closed down the North Beach bars, along with Grover Lewis, a writer for *Rolling Stone Magazine.*

The small press scene in the 60's and 70's provided an environment in which a person could experience literature firsthand. Not academic pretension, but real life. I found myself keeping company with people who not only had a commitment to literature, but were equally committed to social and political causes. It didn't take me long to become an alternative press junkie.

The academic press took few chances, preferring to publish safe and boring poetry. It was left to the alternative press to publish innovative and revolutionary literature. Some of what the alternative press published was good and some of it was bad.

The prestigious literary journals ignored the small press, which published under such outrageous names as *Fuck You, Meatball,* and *The Willie,* edited by a poet who called himself Willie Gobble Cunt. Performance poetry, which is immensely popular today, was represented by poets like Peter Pussy Dog, who frequently appeared on stage dressed in outrageous costumes, along with poets like Mad Dog Max Schwartz and David Moe.

The Meat poets, so named because they wrote about the meat-and-potato issues of the day, began with Charles Bukowski and Douglas Blazek, and quickly spread in popularity thanks to the Mimeo revolution. Nothing was sacred to the Meat poets. Everything constituted poetry: fucking, cursing, drugs, race, prison. It was all the same. Anything and everything was considered poetry. Led by Bukowski, the intent of the Meat poets was to "loosen" the language of poetry. Form was secondary to content. Rhythm and meter, as we know it, was scorned and discarded. While Doug Blazek and others have divorced themselves from Bukowski and the Meat school, hundreds of others remain out there imitating the master (Bukowski). But none of them are remotely capable of matching his success.

I was finding a new world of ideas that had never presented itself to me as a young man who had gone off to serve his country in Panama.

It was in Panama that I first became disillusioned with politics. The President was assassinated at the racetrack. The Vice President was soon arrested for the crime and sent to an island prison without the benefit of a trial. (He would somehow manage to survive the ordeal and later be released.) It was rumored that the Ambassador to the U.S. (later said to be involved in illegal gun running) had been behind the assassination, and the American government (CIA) knew who the real assassin was.

I will always remember the naked children with shacks for homes; ten-year-old boys selling pictures of naked women being fucked by dogs; twelve-year-old prostitutes; taxi drivers pimping for teenage whores, and the fabled "donkey show." Less than a few miles away was the American-controlled Canal Zone with its American Governor, its own U.S. police force, and the life of the privileged class.

By the time I returned home I was already a rebel. I didn't need the Beats to tell me something was wrong with our society. And North Beach would change my life forever.

The little magazines were part of my new world, and in a sense were the missionaries of poetry. In early 1972, I made the decision to publish my own magazine, which later expanded into a small press, publishing over twenty-five books of poetry and anthologies. Alternative literary magazines were referred to as the "littles." Today they are called "zines." Names notwithstanding, the intent of the littles and zines was one and the same: independent, not-for-profit, alternative, literary. The littles, like the zines today, flaunted the establishment's monopoly of the media and distribution networks. It began with the mimeo revolution and ran full course with the evolution of the computer age.

In December 1972, I published the first issue of *Second Coming*. The issue was slick, stapled, and featured mostly small press veteran poets. By design the issue was timeless, with no cover date, copyright, or issue date. This was partly because I wasn't sure there would be a second issue.

When I first started publishing I was pretty naive, despite hanging out with learned small press veterans. I had little or no idea how to accomplish the simplest layout, let alone deal with more complex issues. The first issue, including the typesetting, layout and printing, was done by a small printer in the East Bay who printed literary publications as a sideline to more profitable business activities.

In January 1973, I mailed Hank a copy of the premier issue, and he responded by writing to thank me.

"I had a Second Coming myself the other night," Hank said. "Not bad for a man my age."

This marked the beginning of our friendship. Hank was not the first person to mistake the title of the magazine as a sexual reference. Others mistook the title as a reference to Yeats' poem "The Second Coming." A few people mistook the title for a religious publication. I would sometimes receive trite verse better suited for a bible-belt house organ. These people were all wrong. I chose the name *Second Coming* to signify my commitment to publish the kind of poetry that had influenced my thinking in the 50's and 60's.

Hank thought the first issue placed too much emphasis on prose and not enough on poetry. He said: "In the old days, as much as we looked down on the academy, I remember coming off the park benches into libraries, and reading those phony yet beautiful reviews in the *Kenyon Review*." Hank later sent me two poems for consideration in the second issue, one of which had been accepted but later returned by the *New York Quarterly*. He had strong feelings about the poem and I agreed with his sentiments. He said he would understand if I didn't want to publish it, since it had been rejected by another magazine.

This wasn't a problem for me. It's a sad fact that too many literary magazines refuse to reprint poems. My own belief is that a good poem should appear in as many literary magazines as possible. It's absurd to think a poem should be published only one time, especially in view of the fact that most small literary magazines have little or no distribution. The policy of *Second Coming* was to print anything it considered good, and this included previously published work.

I was only too happy to publish Hank's poem ("Burning in Water"), which appeared in Volume 1, Issue Two of *Second Coming*. I wanted Issue Two to have its own personality. It included artwork, as I began experimenting with matching the written word with the visual. Later issues expanded to include photography paired with specific poems.

Beginning with Issue Two, I became more involved with the magazine, collating several issues and even binding one, thanks to a friend who worked at a local print shop. We would sneak into the shop at night, after the owner had gone home, and use his binding equipment. Hank became a regular contributor and remained the star of the cast up to the time of its demise. I was now toying with the idea of doing a special Bukowski issue, while at the same time learning the trade of small press publishing.

As the magazine evolved, I frequently changed printers as well as the design and format of the magazine to keep it from becoming predictable. It would not be until the fifth issue that *Second Coming* defined its purpose and intent. Dick Ellington, an old-time political activist, became the regular typesetter and layout artist, and Braun/Brumfield became *Second Coming*'s primary printer.

While Hank was the star of the cast, *Second Coming* published many other well-known poets and writers like Philip Levine, Allen Ginsberg, David Meltzer, Charles Plymell, Josephine Miles, Lawrence Ferlinghetti, Harold Norse, James Purdy, Bob Kaufman, Jack Micheline and Ishmael Reed. The magazine also discovered and published poets like Lynne Savitt, Anne Menebroker and Terry Kennedy.

What did I learn about Hank from our meetings, correspondence, and telephone conversations? Perhaps not much more than the avid Bukowski fan already knows. Hank was born in Germany in 1920, the son of an American serviceman and a German national. His parents left Germany when Hank was only three years old, settling in the United States. Hank later attended Los Angeles City College. He endured a bitter relationship with his often abusive father. In his early twenties he wrote a large number of short stories, submitting them to established markets like *Harper's* and the *Atlantic Monthly.* As one might imagine, the stories came back with the usual printed rejection slips.

Like Hank, I too had written hundreds of short stories, submitting them to the very same magazines and received the same standard rejection slips. At one point I had accumulated nearly 200 rejections slips, which I pasted on the walls of my small San Francisco studio apartment. I frequently submitted short stories to the *Evergreen Review* and *Avant Garde Magazine*, but the only success I had was in the early 60's when I sold a short story ("Champ") to the *Mendocino Robin*. I remember the elation I felt when I received the small check and two contributor copies. Shortly afterwards, I sold my first poem for $10 to *Poetry Australia.*

It was around that time I decided to quit writing prose and concentrate on poetry, after receiving a handwritten rejection slip from one of the editors of *Avant Garde Magazine.* Perhaps half in jest, one of the editors had scrawled, "Your style reminds us a lot of Vonnegut, and he's no slouch, but it isn't what the boss is looking for."

The rejection slips were sometimes encouraging and sometimes depressing, but the *Avant Garde* rejection bordered on surrealism, and I wrote a poem about the experience:

Strange Happenings

Avant Garde Magazine
Writes back and says
We like your style a lot
It reminds us a lot
Of Vonnegut
And he's no slouch
But it isn't what
The boss is looking for
And *Esquire* says
We read your work
With interest
But we no longer
Accept unsolicited manuscripts
However we wish you luck
In placing it elsewhere
And then there's
The Chicago Tribune
Who writes and says
Stunning and underlines
It no less.
Not to mention all the others
Who say enjoyed reading your work
Sorry but it's not right for us
But the funniest one of them all
Comes from the friendly local press
Who says absolutely nothing
And sends me back another
Poet's work.

Hank didn't commit himself to poetry until he was thirty-five years old. But in the end it wasn't his poetry, but his prose and screenplay *Barfly* that brought him monetary success. One can only imagine how he must have felt when, in 1944, *Story Magazine* published his first short story. *Story Magazine* (no longer publishing) regularly published writers that Hank admired: Henry Miller, William Saroyan, and Sherwood Anderson. He must have felt he was on the road to success. In the meantime, he continued working at odd jobs while living on the borderline of poverty.

There would be no immediate success for Hank. Following his initial success, neither *Story Magazine* nor other prestigious magazines were eager to publish future short stories. Hank felt that to become a writer he would have to experience life firsthand, and what better place to learn about life than on the streets. He hit the road, much like Jack Kerouac. Only his road included a laundry list of jobs: dishwasher, gas station attendant, stock boy, and a short stint in a slaughterhouse.

In Philadelphia, at the age of 24, he lost his virginity to a woman he met at a bar. Later he returned to Los Angeles, where he began a ten year drinking binge that led him to a Los Angeles hospital charity ward with a bleeding ulcer. During this ten-year period of despair and booze, Hank produced little work, although a few poems appeared sporadically in small magazines.

It was during his search for identity that he met an older woman (Jane Baker) in a skid row bar he frequented. Hank and Jane remained together for several years in a love/hate relationship. Hank drew strength from Jane, and this relationship influenced later poems and short stories. It's probable that Jane, who introduced Hank to the racetrack, was the subject of many of his poems. Living with an alcoholic isn't easy. Two alcoholics living together is a nightmare, one feeding off the weakness of the other. Jane was Hank's first love, and in some ways the affair shaped his relationships with other women.

Several scenes from his screenplay *Barfly* are definitely drawn from Hank's experiences with Jane. Just how important she was to him can be found in "Poem For Jane," one of several poems Hank wrote for her.

After reading Hank's love poem for Jane I realized he was not the hard-boiled person he pretended to be. That Hank built on his "tough guy" image is not surprising. It created a persona that not only worked for him, but also sold books.

There are many myths about Hank, and one of them is that he was the "king of cunnilingus." In an interview with *Rolling Stone,* the interviewer informed him that Linda King said she taught him how to do this, and Hank readily acknowledged that she had. When Hank returned to writing after his ten year search for an identity, he wrote with a vengeance, only this time he concentrated on poetry. But a large number of his poems are little more than prose in disguise. Hank remained a hard boozer despite the fact that doctors warned him it would kill him. He began shotgun mailings of his poems, including several poems to a Texas publication edited and published by a woman named Barbara Frye.

Hank confessed that in one of his many letters to Frye, he jokingly told her of his plans to marry her. He said she later came to Los Angeles and presented him with a marriage proposal. Not long afterwards the two exchanged vows. The marriage took place in Las Vegas, Nevada; hardly the kind of place one might expect Hank to enter into matrimony. But then Hank was never one to conform, and the church was not an institution Hank believed in.

From the start, Hank and Frye had a literary bond. Both possessed huge sexual appetites that helped make the marriage last for several years. But Hank told me Frye possessed a need for middle-class respectability, and that her values conflicted with his own. The marriage never had a chance of succeeding, and ultimately ended in a quiet divorce. But if the marriage was a failure, the experience gave Hank a new wealth of material to draw upon.

Poetry, prose, or screenplays - the theme in Hank's life remained the same. It wasn't until his death that Hank left us with a more conventional piece of writing (*Pulp*) in which his humor truly shines through. It was in the 60's that Hank's reputation began to grow.

In 1960, *Hearse Magazine* published Hank's first book, *Flower, Fist and Beastial Wail.* Hank was on his way to the top, even if it would take many years to get there. It helped that he worked at the post office, which gave him the money to flood the little magazine world with his poetry.

He soon built a following of young readers, partly made possible by the mimeograph revolution, which allowed almost anyone to become a small press publisher. However, Hank wasn't meant for the mimeo revolution, which proved nothing more than an early testing ground.

From the beginning lady luck was with Hank. In the early 60's he met and corresponded with Jon Edgar Webb, owner of LouJon Press and publisher of the esteemed *Outsider Magazine*.

The first issue of *Outsider* appeared in 1961 and featured Henry Miller. The third issue was devoted to Bukowski, and LouJon Press would later publish two beautiful letterpress books of his, *It Catches My Heart In Its Hands* (1963) and *Crucifix in a Deathhand* (1965). It was around this time Hank fathered a daughter named Marina with Frances Smith, whom Hank never married; however, they remained good friends until his death.

I gave a reading at Beyond Baroque and read my poem, "I Paid $3 To See Bukowski Read And Then Went Back Stage And Got In Free." A woman in the back of the room laughed and later encouraged the audience to toss money into a hat she passed around the room. I followed her outside where I thanked her, and watched her get on her bicycle and slowly disappear from view. It wasn't until later that Sandy Garrett, one of the Directors of Beyond Baroque, informed me that the woman was Frances Smith, Marina's mother.

In 1966, Hank began corresponding with Carl Weissner in Germany. Weissner would later translate many of Hank's books into German. Thanks in part to LouJon Press, Hank developed a new audience. Luck was with him when, in spring 1966, Hank met John Martin, who had been impressed with Hank's poem in *The Outsider*. Martin wanted to get into publishing and wanted to start with Bukowski. He soon produced three Bukowski broadsides, paying Hank $30 each. It wasn't long after this that Martin quit his job and began Black Sparrow Press.

In the interim period (1967), Hank formed a friendship with John Bryan, the editor and publisher of several underground newspapers. Bryan convinced Hank to write a weekly column for his newspaper *Open City*. Hank said he received $10 per column, and this was the birth of "Notes of a Dirty Old Man." As *Open City* grew, Bukowski grew with it. The column was hard, honest and appealed to the writing community of the 60's. The newspaper only lasted two years, but it helped propel Bukowski to the forefront of contemporary literature.

In 1968, Martin published his first Black Sparrow book, Hank's *At*

Terror Street and Agony Way. A year later Martin published Hank's *The Days Run Away Like Wild Horses Over the Hills.* That same year Bukowski appeared with Harold Norse and Philip Lamantia in a Penguin Press book, *Modern Poets 13.* Shortly afterwards, Carl Weissner translated N*otes of a Dirty Old Man,* which was published in Germany. 1969 would turn out to be a pivotal year for Hank. It was during this time that Hank began corresponding with Lawrence Ferlinghetti, who later that year published his book *Erections, Ejaculations, Exhibitions, and General Tales of Ordinary Madness.* If it had not been for Hank and Bob Kaufman, I might never have become a poet. It was Hank's ability to expose his own life that made me willing to expose mine, and it was Bob Kaufman who made me realize what it means to be a poet. Hank saw the common worker as ground down and dehumanized by an uncaring social system; a legion of walking dead, made that way by cruel bosses and boring jobs. Writing was his way of beating the system.

It was these early musings, many of which were first published in the *Los Angeles Free Press,* that formed the groundwork for Hank's later novels. Here we encounter Hank's life in the bars, the post office, and as a young man growing up with an abusive father. It's noteworthy that the *Free Press* relegated Hank to its back pages. Bukowski attributed this to the *Free Press* having a large "hippie" audience, whose love-and-peace philosophy was in conflict with Hank's brutal portrayal of life. Hank said this was understandable.

"That's all right. I don't want full approval. I'd rather write the way I want to. Anybody who wants to read me can find me right in front of the sex ads. I kind of soften them up for the sex ads."

It was around the same time that some of my own poems appeared in the back pages of the *Berkeley Barb.* It was easy for me to understand how Hank felt.

As *Second Coming* continued to evolve, so did Hank's work. After twelve years at the post office he decided to quit, after Martin agreed to pay him a small stipend of $200 a month to devote his full time to writing. Much has been made of this brave decision, but the truth is that Hank had saved some money from the sale of the family home willed to him by his father.

He also banked the pension money he received for working those long years at the post office. Still, if Martin had not made his offer to

Hank, he may not have made the decision to quit and work on his first novel (*Post Office*), which he completed in less than three weeks.

Readings were an entirely different matter. Hank hated them, but in 1972 he nevertheless embarked on a series of local readings. The audiences were split. Half the people came to worship and the other half came to heckle. Hank dealt with this by drinking heavily before a reading and was always more than capable of handling the hecklers.

As time passed, *Second Coming* moved in different directions, and I decided to publish the special Charles Bukowski *Second Coming* issue. My intention was to invite both poets and writers, friends and enemies, to provide accounts of their personal experiences with Hank; poems and prose that commented on both the good and bad persona of Bukowski. I wanted a complete portrait of what I considered a complex man. Each contributor was given free rein to choose whatever form they wished. I didn't want the issue to be a "lonelyhearts" project, and felt an equal balance of praise and damnation was necessary. I hoped to show the complexity of a man whom I knew even then was headed for fame.

I wasn't sure if Hank would be interested in the project. However, much to my surprise, he eagerly accepted my invitation and furnished me with a list of potential contributors. I wound up inviting half of Hank's suggested contributors, along with people I knew who had shared experiences with him.

I offered Hank the opportunity to preview what each contributor had said about him and to respond with criticism of his own, but to his credit, he declined. He said, "Let the chips fall where they may."

On January 18, 1973, Hank wrote and said, "I'm honored, if I didn't say so before, to have you put out a special issue on this Bukowski guy." He ended his letter by including the names of several more poets and writers I might want to contact. We continued to exchange letters as the issue progressed. Hank asked if I would consider publishing a short story he had earlier published in another magazine, but I felt the special issue would be better served with original material. In the end, I did republish "Six Inches," one of Hank's more famous short stories. When I paid him a small amount of money, he wrote back and said, "You're the last of the devil's honest men." He enclosed a stunning personal photograph which I later used for the front cover of the special issue. As the months passed Hank became impatient, but promised to send me a long statement which he felt would have more value than a short story.

"I'll get a couple bottles of wine and sit down at the typer. We'll get many imperfections this way, but I'm not against imperfections.

"I think the literary people are too smooth, too careful. Piss on that. It's my old ass that is going to get exposed."

Hank's rambling essay ("He Beats His Women"), which I used in the special Bukowski issue, was later published in the *Pushcart Press Anthology*, and sold by John Martin to a German publishing house.

Not long after receiving Hank's letter I came across an issue of Len Fulton's *Small Press Review,* which featured several poets commenting on Bukowski and his work. I was curious how Hank felt about what had been said about him in *SPR*. He wrote back and said: "I think the *Small Press Review* was a hatchet job, with Fulton leading the tribe. I don't mind Harold Norse. He's basically honest and strung out. It's just that his eyes, or whatever he sees out of, have it wrong."

On Fulton, I knew Hank was wrong. I've known Len for nearly thirty years, and he is a fair and objective editor and publisher. For the first time I began to see that while Hank could dish out criticism, he was thin-skinned about receiving it. Hank's main criticism with *Small Press Review* was it had too many poets/writers "with a bitch to grind." Hank felt these writers were trying to build careers at his expense and that too much time was spent on people like this. Talking about them only gave them what they wanted and needed. Hank said it was okay to be attacked and he expected a certain amount of it, but that it was seldom honest. He said, in part:

"Long ago, when I first started writing poems at the age of 35, I knew that when I got these writers angry I was getting there."

In a later letter, Hank told me to say hello to his tormentors from the North, whom he identified only by their initials (H.N. and J.B.), whom I knew to be Harold Norse and John Bryan. He said:

"Tell them that I'm not dead yet, and that I'll be back with more poems and stories to jam down their throats, and another novel (*Factotum*) and maybe a play."

Hank said he had reservations about writing the play, but said he could use the thousand dollar advance he had been offered. He said he needed more time to think about it.

"I don't like actors and directors and I don't like stages. The way they look or the way they work. There's not much that I like, and I like less and less each day."

In October 1973, I wrote Hank and informed him of an encounter I had with Jack Micheline. Micheline told me he was "pissed" at Hank because he had paid him a visit in Los Angeles in the hope Hank might help him get a manuscript published, only to have Hank give him the "cold shoulder." Hank wrote back and said Jack's work was fine, but Jack had caught him at the wrong time, under the wrong circumstances. Hank felt Jack too often went off on what Hank referred to as the "I'm-a-poet" trip, and that this attitude took away from Jack's work.

"Like, poor bastard, he's a poet. Well, there are a lot of poor bastard hospital interns, farmhands, garbage collectors, dishwashers, factory workers . . . if anybody has divine rights, they probably have them too."

Micheline was upset at what Bukowski said. I had known Micheline for nearly two decades, up until the time of his death in 1998. I knew him to be a deeply sensitive person who often hid behind a brash front. His admiration and respect for Bukowski was evident from the time I first met him.

Micheline was of Russian-Rumanian Jewish ancestry. He was a true Bronx poet and, although he often said he didn't consider himself a member of the Beat generation, his work speaks to the Beat era. Jack was an interesting person; a friend of James T. Farrell, William Saroyan, Langston Hughes and jazz musicians like Charlie Mingus.

He regularly read his poetry in cafes and bars, accompanied by jazz musicians. The only poets who could read their work to jazz as well as Micheline were Bob Kaufman and Kenneth Patchen.

If Micheline screamed "poet" too often and too loud, it was only because he was largely ignored by the literary establishment. Like Hank, Micheline's work spoke to the down and out; the misfits of society, the dopers, hookers, homosexuals and destitute population that the majority of our society turns its back on. Micheline's firsthand knowledge of the streets and the people who live there rivaled that of Bukowski. He took to the road at the young age of seventeen, when he enlisted in the military. By the time he was nineteen, he found himself in Israel. Then it was back to the United States to work a variety of odd jobs, and traveling à la Kerouac's *On the Road.*

Part of the Greenwich Village Beat movement in the 50's, Micheline identified himself with street poet Maxwell Bodenheim. He saw the poet as a revolutionary whose purpose is to free people from stifling jobs and relationships. He believed the poet's job is to live poetry and set a fearless example for others. In this, his philosophy differed from Bukowski, but their writing shared much in common.

Hank told me that when Micheline was "on," even he (Bukowski) couldn't touch him. This is high praise coming from someone considered by many to be one of the best writers since World War Two. Micheline's first book of poetry, *River of Red Wine*, was reviewed favorably by Dorothy Parker.

During his Beat days in New York, he often walked the streets with Jack Kerouac. While his work might not stand up to Hank's overall contribution to literature, he was second to none as an oral poet. In a July 1993 letter to Bukowski, Micheline talks to Hank in a part-prose/part-poem commentary:

> **I know you're going through changes man**
> **I feel them out here**
> **I don't write often and it's okay to use each other**
> **That's what it should be all about.**

And in a letter to Micheline, Hank said:

"You ain't been forgotten man. Neeli and I, anyhow, talk about you often, and I wrote a couple of poems for you, one titled 'Looking For Jack Micheline.' Forget the other one, but no bad slams. Your letters are poems."

Nowhere was Micheline's love for Hank more evident than in a long free verse poem in the *Second Coming* Charles Bukowski issue entitled "Long After Midnight."

> **he is one of the finest poets writing and breathing today**
> **he is the beer bottle**
> **he is Quasimodo**
> **he is stone face himself**
> **he is the freak of L.A.**
> **he is the hunchback of Hollywood Boulevard**
> **he is kind to his daughter**

he is kind to his daughter
he is kind to his daughter
all he is folks is a glass of water
and the longest shot that ever came home.

To those who attacked Hank and his work without ever knowing the man, Micheline's lines "he is kind to his daughter" refer to the loving, sensitive side of Hank. A side Hank didn't often show to the outside world. Suffice it to say Hank and Micheline had a special friendship that transcended their different philosophies. Micheline saw poetry as a holy message to be delivered to the masses while Hank saw poetry as just another job, no different from a carpenter or electrician with certainly nothing holy about it.

But the dark side of Hank was there too. When Micheline began publishing his short stories, Hank wrote and told me Micheline should stick to writing poetry and forget about short story writing, referring to his prose as "buttermilk." He suggested someone should tell Micheline to stick to poetry, where his real talent lay. I foolishly passed this information on to Micheline and he became furious. He mistakenly believed I was expressing my own viewpoint and subsequently wrote one of the most vicious letters I have ever received. It all became water under the bridge when I later published his collection of short stories entitled *Skinny Dynamite*.

I'm not sure what Hank's intentions were, but he was wrong about Micheline. His short story writing fell short of Bukowski's best work, but his style was pure Micheline. He had a straightforward approach to telling a story in an easy and insightful manner.

Eight

On Saint Patrick's Day in 1973 I was drinking heavily at the 1232 Club, also known as The Saloon. Earlier in the day Micheline had stopped by to drop off a long prose poem which focused on the loss of the American dream. It was an impressive poem that made an instant impression on me. He joined me for a drink at the bar and I soon found myself agreeing to publish the poem in *Second Coming.*

After Micheline left the bar I sat at one of the corner tables and read the poem several times. By late afternoon I had consumed several shots of Jack Daniels and was feeling no pain. It was growing dark outside when Wayne Miller, a young North Beach poet, came into the bar with Micheline and asked me if I wanted to go to a party at the Petri Art School. Wayne was popular with the women in North Beach and headed the weekly poetry readings at the Coffee Gallery. He taught an art class at the nearby San Francisco Art Institute, and was a talented poet in his own right.

The three of us chatted for a few minutes before I accompanied them outside, where we managed to flag down a passing taxi. We climbed into the back seat of the cab and settled back for the short ride to the school. Micheline and Miller engaged in an intense conversation. I had no idea I was heading for a trip I would remember for the rest of my life. When we arrived at the party it was going full blast, complete with psychedelic lights, topless young women and an assortment of artists, writers, and bohemians dancing and drinking the night away.

I was stoned out of my mind and only vaguely recall Miller warning me not to drink from the punch bowl, which was spiked with LSD. At the time, my experience with drugs was limited to marijuana, uppers, downers, and one trip on opium. I'm sure if I had been sober I would have realized that alcohol and LSD is a dangerous mix. I ignored Miller's warning and drank a full plastic cup of spiked punch. What followed was a living nightmare. I remember staggering down the stairs and stumbling outside into the street. Everything was a blur.

Passing strangers seemed to be wearing masks. I could hear acid rock music from the upstairs party, only the sound was completely distorted.

Here I was standing on the streets of my hometown, a major player in what would turn out to be a bad horror movie. Everything seemed to be moving in slow motion, and people seemed to be talking at half speed. I clutched Micheline's manuscript in my hands, trying desperately to hail a taxi to take me back to my home turf in North Beach.

If you have ever been in San Francisco on a busy weekend night, catching a taxi can be like winning the lottery. I was walking familiar streets, but might as well have been in Russia. I'm not sure when I spotted the double-parked cab with the keys in the ignition. I looked to my left and saw the cab driver was assisting an elderly couple into the lobby of a nearby hotel. I jumped into the front seat of the taxi, put the car in gear, and drove off in the direction of North Beach. My crazed mind told me I could leave the cab in North Beach and later call the taxi company and tell them where to come and pick it up. The idea was insane, but in my chemically impaired state of mind it seemed perfectly proper. That I was committing a felony never crossed my mind. The deed done, I found myself racing down the street. The world was mine. At some point (according to the police report), I turned the wrong way into a one way street. I was too stoned to see the "Do Not Enter" sign, which was clearly visible to a normal person.

I'm not sure when I heard the police siren or first saw the flashing red lights of the police car. I only know at some point my brain returned to normal. I found myself slowing down and pulling over to the curb. I half staggered, half fell out of the cab, stumbling over to the two police officers who had parked their cruiser behind the cab. My fogged mind told me this was Saint Patrick's Day, and the officers would surely see the humor behind this desperate act. I mean, who in their right mind would steal a taxi and for what purpose?

The two cops jumped from their cruiser. The cop on the passenger side had his gun drawn. It was as if they had cornered a bank robber. I wanted to explain the whole damn thing but the expressions on their faces were serious and threatening.

"Don't move, you son-of-a-bitch," the cop with the moustache said, his gun pointed at me. The other cop moved behind me, wrestling me to the ground, quickly handcuffing my hands behind my back. I found myself roughly pushed back up on my feet and thrown against the side of the squad car. One of the cops frisked me for weapons while his partner kept his gun pointed at me.

"He's clean," I heard one of the cops say.

I tried my best to explain the situation, only to hear the cop with the moustache say "Shut your fucking mouth if you know what's good for you." I was put in the back seat of the cruiser and made to sit there for what seemed like an eternity. Finally a second police car arrived at the scene. I watched an overweight Police Sergeant get out of his patrol car and talk to the two arresting police officers. The Sergeant walked over to the cruiser and peered through the back window. It reminded me of a scene I had seen many times on television police shows.

"Book him," I heard the Sergeant say. I watched him walk over to his patrol car and drive away. It was like watching a re-run of "Hawaii-Five-O." The two arresting police officers started their car up and drove off in the direction of the Central Police Station. I was being taken to North Beach, but not in the manner I had hoped. The cop on the passenger side of the police car glanced back at me. "Is your name Micheline?" he asked. He was reading from Jack's manuscript that he had taken from me.

"No," I said. I never got to finish the sentence as the cop turned to his partner and said, "Fucking Commie. Listen to this shit." The officer began reading a passage from Micheline's poem. A long stanza about how America is not the dream it's cracked up to be. He read, "I see the tongues of dogs in America. Every day they murder poets in America." The cop on the passenger side of the car reached back and slammed the divider window shut. It was obvious they didn't want to hear from me. To them I was scum and Commie scum at that.

I was driven to the basement of the North Beach Central Precinct Station and administered a field sobriety test before being taken to a holding cell. It seemed like hours before I was transported to City Prison where I was booked on a Felony One charge of auto theft and driving under the influence of a controlled substance. The booking officer joked to a fellow jailer:

"Who booked this guy on a Felony One?" he asked no one in particular. "Sounds like something I'd do."

I was not allowed to make a telephone call until I was stripped naked and inspected like a piece of meat. I was told to bend over and "spread them." And then I felt a gloved finger invade my ass as male and female officers freely passed by, some of them booking prisoners of their own. I remembered seeing a woman on television talking about the demeaning experience of being strip-searched, and now it was happening to me.

I don't think I'll ever forget the holding cell filled with the dredges of humanity. Most of the men had been there before and knew what to expect. They seemed resigned to their fate. There was an eerie silence, as if each of them were going through their own private hell. I quickly learned you either sack out on one of the wooden benches or lie on the floor, waiting with countless other lost souls to hear your name called. Waiting to become part of the criminal index system that will remain with you for the rest of your life. But not before you are stripped, pushed up against a wall, and told to spread your cheeks, while a jailer shines a small flashlight up your ass searching for hidden contraband. I later read an essay by Hank that appeared in *Nola Express,* which told the story of his being arrested for a DUI by the Los Angeles police. There were similarities to my own San Francisco arrest. Hank said:

"No bunks, thirty-five men lying on the floor. There were a couple of urinals and a couple of toilets. Most of the men were Mexican and most of the Mexicans were between forty and sixty-five. There were two blacks. No Chinese. I have never seen a Chinese man in a drunk tank."

Hank talked about a Mexican being brought into the cell who was in need of medical attention. Hank yelled to the guards that the man needed assistance. "There's a guy in here who needs medical attention," Hank cried out. The guards just kept walking about, doing their duties.

"Listen, do you guys hear me?" Hank asked. "There's a man in here who needs attention real bad." There was still no response. Hank said the guards seemed totally disinterested, just going about their daily business.

Hank talked about being in the holding tank. "Those of us who have money, we bail out, we get fined. The money we pay is used to enable them to arrest us again. Now, I mean, if you want to call that justice, you can call it justice. I call it shit down the throat."

That may be as political as Hank ever got. In contrast to Hank's situation, the felony wing at San Francisco City Prison defied description. There were cots lined up like you might find in an army barracks.

One filthy toilet and one filthy wash basin. If you had to take a leak or crap, you did it in front of twenty or thirty men. Just one of many plans designed to beat your psyche down.

I was only one of three whites in the cell. No one talks to you here. The old pros size you up. They can tell you're not one of them. You're a duck in a lion's cage. You're a white man walking alone in Harlem at 3 a.m. You're a misdemeanor among felons. You simply haven't paid your dues. There were thieves and pimps and suspected murderers sprinkled in with one felony auto theft and a small-time drug user or two. You guard your spare change like it's gold. It buys cigarettes and favors and men have been killed for less.

The first person to talk to me was a man in his late thirties. He looked every bit the part of a criminal. The kind you've seen in old George Raft movies. He talked about how he had killed his girlfriend, and wanted to know what I had been arrested for. I tried to puff up the felony auto theft but I was nothing more than a punk to him. I watched him shake his head as he walked back to his bunk. Not long afterwards a tough-looking Latino male approached me. He reminded me of the gang members in the Mission District: short, dark hair, moustache, all muscles. He held out a subway token, wanting to exchange it for the spare change I had.

"I don't have any use for a subway token," I said, looking him straight in the face. I'm sure he saw through the false bravado. He never cracked a smile, flashing a half-menacing look before retreating to the other end of the cell. I would occasionally see him looking my way, a smirk on his face. His eyes were hard steel, and I began to fear for my safety. I had no idea what to expect if forced to spend the weekend in confinement. I imagined the worst!

I lay back on an empty bunk but found it impossible to sleep. The alcohol was racing through my veins and my heart was pounding with anxiety. I lay there silently watching the men in blue go about their business. A guard walked by, peering inside the cell, showing little if any emotion. If there had been no drunk Chinese in Hank's cell, there was a sober Chinese seaman in the felony wing. He spoke limited English.

"Phone call, Sir. Phone call, Sir!" These words were repeated over and over again until I thought I would go mad. The guards ignored him. The man had been allowed his one telephone call and it was his bad luck to have dialed the wrong number. There was no room for mistakes with these men in blue. The blacks understood this best. They were not new to the situation. Most of them had been there before and would return again. They asked for and received no favors.

As I said, it's hard to describe the felony wing. If you've ever visited a zoo, it might be compared to an animal enclosure with keepers passing by and peering at you. There are too many men confined in too small a space. A mattress and a blanket for each army-type bunk. There is the noise and shouting that never abates. Some of the blacks sang to help pass the time, but mostly it was just a constant chatter that never seemed to stop. It's hard for the quiet ones to cope. You just lie there trying to sort things out inside your head with the noise of a hundred conversations going on at the same time.

I asked one of the guards what time it was, and when he told me it was 4 p.m., I began to panic. I had used my allotted phone call to post bail. The bondsman told me he would try to find a judge, who was out on the golf course, to sign the necessary papers. If he couldn't locate the judge by 5 p.m., I would have to spend the weekend in jail. A civilian pharmacist stopped by the cell, dispensing medication. Lunch was served late. They were shooting a scene for a movie, *The Laughing Cop* or some other absurd name, and the men in confinement began to yell at their keepers.

I remained silent. Suddenly a key turned in the door and a trustee in blue jeans and a white frock entered the cell, pushing a meal cart. We were served cold cuts, two pieces of bread, lukewarm split pea soup, black coffee, water, and jello. I nibbled at the food, not really hungry. My attention was drawn to two burly men approaching the Chinese illegal immigrant. I watched them take away his tray and scoop the food onto their own trays, leaving him with nothing but the cup of cold coffee and soup. The Chinese man knew better than to protest. I was becoming increasingly anxious, imagining the Latino sneaking over to my bunk during the night and taking my change, or worse yet, doing me bodily harm. A young black man, who appeared equally apprehensive, came over and struck up a conversation. He had been arrested for possession of marijuana after being pulled over by the police for having a defective taillight. We entered into an alliance to come to the aid of the other if one of us were attacked.

I thought of what was happening outside, which only made matters worse. I had visions of my friends getting drunk in North Beach. Young women looking to get laid. Sad faces in lonely hotel rooms staring at the four walls. The 1232 Club would soon be gearing up for the mad-hatter night crowd.

Finally, at ten minutes to five, a guard opened the cell door and yelled, "Bail." The young black man had been bailed out thirty minutes earlier.

"Get out here on the double," the guard shouted, calling my name. I started to leave the cell when the guard suddenly stuck out a hand and pushed it hard against my chest, causing me to stumble backwards.

"Where's your blanket?" the guard asked. "What the fuck is wrong with you?"

I went back to the bunk and retrieved the blanket. Angry, but with a trace of my manhood restored, I tossed the blanket in the guard's hamper.

"You want the damn blanket, then ask for it," I said.

The guard looked at me with hatred and I knew that was not a wise remark. His eyes seemed to say "Next time your ass is mine." I could only hope there would be no next time.

My release from City Prison occurred after the property room had closed for the weekend, which meant I was unable to pick up my belongings until the next work day. The all-business but kindly bail bondsman lent me the money to take a cab home. Outside the sky was painter blue. Everything seemed beautiful to me. I remember thinking that it takes time in the slammer to make you realize just how valuable freedom is.

Two weeks later I appeared in court before a stern judge who never looked at me during the entire proceeding. I gave my lawyer permission to plead me guilty to a reduced misdemeanor charge of driving an automobile without the owner's consent and driving under the influence of alcohol. The judge sentenced me to a ninety-day suspended jail sentence and eighteen months probation. I went downstairs to the probation department, where I was interviewed by a young probation officer who read my case file with an amused look.

"What the hell is this?" the probation officer asked, more to himself than me. "You aren't going to do something crazy like this again, are you?"

"No," I told him.

"I'm not going to require you to come in for regular visits," he said. "Just make sure you stay out of trouble."

"What about the judge?" I asked.

"I'll take care of that," the probation officer said. "I'm putting you on court probation."

"What's that?" I asked.

"It means you don't have to report to me, but if you come before the court again anytime in the next eighteen months, you'll serve the full eighteen months in jail." He extended his hand and wished me luck, walking back to his office. I took the elevator downstairs to the front lobby.

On the ride downstairs I thought about the lawyer I had hired to represent me. He was an ex-San Francisco police officer who had been forced to take an early retirement because he was an alcoholic. I paid him $800 to work out a plea bargain. Not bad for a half-day's work. The system takes care of its own. Getting off the elevator, I thought about the young Assistant District Attorney and how he smiled at me after the judge had meted out my sentence. His words were like a bullet to my head.

"Don't take it personally, kid. It looks good on the records."

After making bail I wrote Hank and told him the special Bukowski issue might be delayed because of the fine and legal fees I had incurred. I assured him the issue would be published, but I couldn't give him a firm date. Hank wrote back and said:

"You've been battered, ripped and jailed, and still can get it together to get an issue out about another fucked-up human being. That takes something that has a touch of the holy, and I want you to know that I know it."

Hank's letter was filled with words of encouragement and helped see me through a difficult time in my life. In a subsequent letter I told him I had no one but myself to blame for my Saint Patrick's Day arrest, for ignoring Wayne Miller's warning not to drink from the LSD-spiked punch bowl. He wrote back and said:

"Sounds like you did it up, but there you go, it's the price and pain of drinking and it's like the price and pain of women.

"You've got to pay hard sometimes when you least expect it. I've been in so much trouble. Jail, jail, jail, jail, jail, jail, jail, jail and fine, fine and jail; drunk driving, getting beat up while drunk. All that, well, it's the same for most of us, but one of the best things I have learned is to stay out of the bars and try to stay off the street. I fail sometimes to stay off the streets, but not too often."

I talked to Hank about wanting to be left alone for awhile. I just didn't want to see or hear from anyone but wasn't sure he would understand. His reaction: "Some real dead creeps over last night, brought no energy, and I had to split for the beer though there were four of them. Taken again. They ate my time. Nothing to do. They had nothing to do, and there are billions just like them." I knew full well what Hank meant. I had experienced the same thing, but with different players.

One of the finest poems Hank wrote touched on this very subject, "Don't Come Around But If You Do." I would later publish the poem in *Second Coming*. In the poem he speaks about the poet just trying to keep himself alive a bit longer, and when someone knocks unannounced at the door, maybe hears a noise inside and the poet doesn't answer, that maybe it just wasn't meant to be.

In subsequent exchanges of letters, Hank and I discussed drinking and the affect alcohol has on the body. Hank told me to try and stay off the booze but admitted he had trouble following his own advice. In one of his letters he spun a tale about a woman who let him out of her car in the middle of the freeway, late in the evening, in a bad part of town. There was no public transportation and he had been forced to walk to a liquor store to purchase a pint of liquor, and shared it with the cab driver who later joined him on a two-day drinking binge. In another letter, Hank talked about his mad-hatter life with women.

"Got a new jacket ripped to pieces by this crazy woman. The problem of wandering the streets at night is mainly the cops, but also others who are out there too." He closed his letter by saying, "I suppose a few of my fellow poets up there are bad-mouthing me. If those bastards only put as much energy into their poetry as they did into their own gossip, they would be the geniuses they pretend themselves to be."

I managed to recover from my Saint Patrick's Day arrest.

In December 1973 I mailed Hank the proof for the front cover of the Special Bukowski issue. Hank wrote back with his approval, "All grace, she looks good." Along with the proof of the cover I expressed my feelings on how hard it was to meet someone for the first time, remembering how this had not been the case with him. Most people consider me an extrovert but I'm often quiet with people I meet for the first time.

Hank said, "Yes it's hard to meet, but glad you weren't the holy and precious finicky poet type. There's a certain mold that most of those babes seem to fill. You looked more like a movie tough with a taste for the next drink."

In a telephone conversation Hank talked about how he had gone to the mailbox earlier in the day and found a literary magazine with a lengthy poetry essay by an English teacher and lecturer, who was a poet of some reputation. Hank said that after reading the essay he felt the professor wrote badly and without any feeling.

"He writes about nothing with great tenacity, and follows most of it up with organic matter theories and much dead and stilted terminology which, like his art, almost seems to say something if you scratch long and hard enough, and you can mouth a lot of bullshit about that too."

Hank said he instantly trashed the magazine article and that what he found particularly offensive was a remark the professor had made.

"Now maybe my troubles are your troubles too."

Hank felt the professor had stolen a statement repeated on street corners long ago and was pulling a "damned two-bit hoax."

Hank said, "His troubles are not my troubles. He has chosen against troubles and to die. I have chosen trouble and to live." Hank believed if a person had the choice between being a professor and a dishwasher, he should take the dishwashing job without hesitation.

I shared Hank's disdain for the academic crowd. In 1962, I enrolled at San Francisco State College, where I had earlier received a BA degree in Sociology. My intention was to earn a post-graduate degree in creative writing.

San Francisco State is now a University but remains a relatively small campus, with a medium-sized student population. At the time of my enrollment the creative writing department had a reputation for being one of the best in the country, but I dropped out of the graduate program in less than six weeks.

I signed up for two courses: "Introduction to Creative Writing" and "Introduction to the Short Story." The first class was taught by the late William Dickey. If I had known what was in store for me that first day in class, I would not have bothered to show up.

Nine

The first day of class I arrived early and took a seat near the front of the room. Shortly afterwards a man with a goatee and carrying a briefcase took a seat in the front row. I watched him open his briefcase and take out a writing pad. He seemed heavy in thought when I approached him. I introduced myself and asked if he was taking the class too. The man turned and flashed me a cold look.

"I'm teaching the class," he said. I tried to avoid looking him in the face as the other students arrived. The man closed his briefcase and moved to the blackboard behind the teaching podium. He picked up a piece of chalk and wrote in large letters: Introduction to Creative Writing. Professor Dickey.

Dickey informed us that he didn't want anyone writing in the style of Jack Kerouac. I raised my hand and asked why. Dickey replied that Kerouac wasn't a "legitimate writer." I was too stunned to pursue the subject further.

The short story class was different. I don't recall the name of the teacher who taught it. He was an attractive man, the kind young coeds fall in love with. The man possessed a pleasant personality. What struck me most was a young student barely out of his teens, who raised his hand and proclaimed that he found F. Scott Fitzgerald's metaphors "outdated." The bell rang before the professor had time to respond. As I left I found myself wondering what I was doing in a classroom of students all much younger than me.

Back in Dickey's class, a second incident occurred which ended my interest in pursuing a creative writing degree. Not content to put down Kerouac's writing, Dickey began to dissect the work of John Steinbeck. His comments were less than favorable. Again I raised my hand and asked him what he found wrong with Steinbeck's work. He said, "I suppose I just don't like people who write books about travels with their dogs."

Shortly before the class ended we were handed an assignment to write a story in dialogue. Over the weekend I copied two pages of dialogue from an F. Scott Fitzgerald short story. The following Monday I went to the counselor's office and completed a class dropout card. I had decided to drop Dickey's class but wanted to leave on my own terms. I attended the next scheduled class and handed in the assignment, knowing it would be my last one. Two days later I returned to Dickey's class, curious to see his reaction to the paper I had turned in. I had not yet handed in my class dropout card but there was no turning back. I watched Dickey walk up the aisle handing back each student's paper, glaring at me as he returned my paper. In bold red lettering was a red circled "F," with a notation for me to see him after class.

I'll always remember the look of anger on his face when he confronted me, demanding to know what made me think I could get away plagiarizing the work of F. Scott Fitzgerald.

I looked him straight in the face and said, "Quite frankly, I didn't think you'd know the difference." Dickey was beside himself with anger.

"I think you had better drop my class," he fumed.

"I already have," I said, handing him the dropout card. This would be my last contact with San Francisco State College, except to return years later as a guest poet.

Hank found my experience amusing. In a telephone conversation he said he had undergone a similar experience, having enrolled in journalism classes at Los Angeles City College, but dropped out for much the same reasons I had.

Hank said that during this same period in his life he had enrolled in a creative writing class, but the teacher immediately turned him off. He said, "The guy was a damn dork. It was tea and cookies and students at his feet on a soft rug. If that's poetry, then I'm a striped-assed baboon."

It was during a telephone conversation that I learned of Hank's love for classical music. As we talked I could hear Brahms playing in the background. Some people believe music soothes the beast in man, but I never personally saw the beast in Hank. When Hank was sober he could be unbelievably shy. A man who listened more than he talked.

Many of Hank's friends and casual acquaintances had this media image of a caveman, belching in public while looking up skirts of young women. In truth, Hank was a sensitive man. A poet and writer who penned some of the best poetry and prose of our time. Most of his work was written while sitting behind his typewriter listening to the classical masters. How much Handel, Bach, Mozart, Beethoven, Mahler and Brahms influenced Hank's work no one can say for sure. It is fairly safe to say serious music was a central part of his life.

This isn't hard for me to understand. I have always believed poetry and music are intricate parts of each other. With the Beat poets it was Jazz. With me it was Edith Piaff, the legendary French singer. I don't speak French and can't understand a word she is singing, but her voice is pure poetic magic.

Billie Holiday is another singer who helped me through low points in my life. I remember getting off the night shift at the post office and walking across the street to a corner bar. The bartender was a punch drunk ex-boxer named Carl who liked to tell stories about his days in the ring. It was a welcome relief from the brain-killing hours at the post office, sorting dirty sacks into three feet high piles, the black soot sticking to the hairs in my nostrils. But even here I couldn't escape the post office, as workers floated in and out for a quick drink or two in order to help see them through the long night.

I'd joke with Carl and listen to the sad tunes on the old jukebox, waiting for the day when I would be able to put the post office behind me. My brain cells overloaded on the sheer stupidity of the supervisors and foremen who, hating their own misery, seemed to find it necessary to make your life as miserable as their own.

I was more often than not half drunk by the time I rode the Mission Street bus home. Once home I'd pop open a can of beer, lie back on the bed, and turn on an old Billie Holiday record. And so it was with Bukowski. While the masters played their magic on the radio, Hank created his own magic on the typewriter, momentarily putting the demons to rest.

Hank and I continued to correspond with each other. When someone told him Micheline was badmouthing him, he wrote and told me he bore no grudges, and that he understood.

"Micheline is all right," he said. "He's one-third bullshit, but he's got a special strength."

Hank felt that Jack's strength was weakened by his insistence that the poet was a holy man, but believed that his work outweighed his weakness. Hank said:

"I like the way his lines roll and flow. His poems are total feelings beating their head upon barroom floors. He comes closer to a sooth-sayer, the gambler, the burner of the stinking buckskin than any man I've known."

Not long afterwards, Hank wrote about his break-up with Linda King. He complained that women were both a curse and a salvation. He was upset over the fact King had accused him of turning her into an alcoholic. He vehemently denied this, telling me he was fortunate to have the classical masters to see him through the bad times he was going through.

Hank said "Well, there's still the beer and a rolled cigarette and my radio plays a touch of Brahms."

For Linda King's part, she said that when she met Hank he hadn't been around a woman for four years, and that she intentionally teased and turned him on during a sitting for a bust she did of him at her home in Los Angeles. She had Hank pegged for a caveman until one night he wrote her the most beautiful love letter she had ever received from a man. Linda said Hank continued to write her love letters and love poems until she finally fell in love with him. The two-plus years Hank and Linda spent together were filled with love and war, with Linda claiming that if she told Hank not to do something, he'd go out and do it just to prove his superiority. The split between them was inevitable and not on the best of terms.

As time passed I thought I detected a certain disinterest on Hank's part concerning the *Second Coming* Charles Bukowski issue. I be-lieved Hank thought the issue might never come about. I expressed my feelings in a letter to him. He wrote back and said:

"I know I haven't been fired-up over your Buk issue, but I'm quiet in things of this nature, and just because I don't storm your door with tons of green beer doesn't mean I don't feel the honor or feel good about it." He went on to discuss some bad times he was experiencing, while at the same time acknowledging my own hard times. He told me he appreciated the sacrifices I was making in time and money to get the issue out. He said:

"You're in the bullring. I see you there, and it's charging down. We assume so much. We all get down low at times. Let me say that I understand, and will try to get more work to you soon. Something that will fit into our bullring where they have us crazy and lunging and gambling, but not quitting."

Hank's letter helped lift my spirits. I wrote back and told him that after reading his prose piece "He Beats His Women," I didn't need any additional work for the issue. His statement on women was a strong one, and I believed a fitting piece to close the issue with. He seemed relieved to learn he would not have to send me any more work. He wrote back and said, "Winans, you write a letter like a man who knows where it's at."

In his letter, he went on to talk about his hero (and mine), Lefty O'Doul, who had played for and managed the old San Francisco Seals baseball team. Lefty was a legend in San Francisco. A phenomenal hitter who never made the Hall of Fame because he didn't play the required 1000 games, having played but 970 major league baseball games. He nevertheless gained fame as one of the most feared hitters in the game, from his rise as a San Francisco Seal through his 1920 season with the Philadelphia Phillies, when he hit for a .398 average.

When I was growing up, the San Francisco Seals were an outstanding Triple A baseball team. One of the local favorites was Roy Nicely, who played shortstop. Nicely was a Golden Glove ballplayer but had trouble hitting .200, which doomed him to the minor leagues for his entire career. Lefty O'Doul, like most of the Seal's ballplayers in those days, had his telephone number listed in the local directory. One afternoon I put a towel over the phone, trying to sound older, and telephoned his home. When he answered the phone and identified himself, I asked him why he didn't replace Nicely with a ballplayer who could hit for a higher average.

"Why don't you go to hell," Lefty said, slamming the telephone down. No one told O'Doul how to manage his team.

O'Doul was a colorful figure in San Francisco, managing the Seals after his playing days in the major leagues were over. After he retired from baseball he bought a bar and named it after himself. He became famous for serving drinks on one side of the bar and starting fights on the other. He was what San Francisco was all about in those days, and I could see why he appealed to Hank.

In earlier correspondence I had told Hank about my experience as a kid when I played pickup baseball games with Joe Sprinz, a former catcher for the San Francisco Seals, who pitched slow ball for both sides.

Sprinz's son had a crippled arm yet played the outfield, and played it well. He would catch a fly ball in his gloved hand, drop the glove, switch the ball to his good hand, and throw it accurately back to the infield. He did this so gracefully that no one thought of him as having a handicap. Even with only one good arm he hit for a better average than many of the kids. Practically weaned on Lefty O'Doul and Joe Sprinz, I ate and breathed baseball, dreaming of one day becoming another Joe DiMaggio or Ted Williams.

In his letter Hank said, "Even at fifty, I remember Lefty pinch-hitting against the Los Angeles Angels."

Hank went on to marvel at how Lefty more often than not always seemed to get a hit. "But like you," he said, "all that has drained out of me."

Reading Hank's letter I flashed back to my own childhood. I can't recall how old I was when my father took me to Seals Stadium to see my first baseball game, but the memory is as fresh as yesterday. My father didn't drive, so we took the streetcar to the ballpark. It was the first time I had been inside Seals Stadium, which was located on 16th and Bryant Street near the old Southern Pacific Railway tracks. I stood proudly at my father's side as he bought two tickets at one of the ticket counters. I was amazed at the hundreds of people walking through the gates into the stadium. Inside, the park was filled with excitement. Men selling programs. Hot dog and coke stands. Men in colorful uniforms, walking up the aisles and yelling, "Hot dogs, peanuts, Cracker Jacks." We had good seats behind home plate, and I remember thinking how green the ballfield was.

The home town Seals were on the field taking batting practice. I watched in awe as Dino Restelli and others hit long fly balls into the bleachers. There were my heroes yelling things like "hubba-hubba," dressed in their white striped uniforms. Then the umpire was yelling "Play Ball" and the Seals took the field to loud applause. They were playing the hated cross-town rivals, the Oakland Oaks. I stuffed myself with hotdogs and peanuts and coke, standing up for the seventh inning stretch as the organist played "Take Me Out To The Ball Game."

I cheered when the crowd cheered. I jeered at the home plate umpire when the crowd yelled at him for making a wrong call. The Seals lost that day, but it didn't matter. It was the most exciting day of my childhood, and I was hooked on baseball. But time has a way of eroding the past. Today the national pasttime has become a game with ego-driven ballplayers with multi-million dollar contracts. The Seals are a fading memory. Perhaps the dream ended even earlier, the day my father said he couldn't take time off from his job to take me to the annual "Father and Son" baseball game. I was embarrassed to have my mother take me to the game.

The Seals were playing an exhibition game against the Cleveland Indians, and Bob Feller was on the mound. The ever-present weak-hitting Roy Nicely would remember this day too, but for far different reasons, somehow managing to hit a long double off of Feller.

As fate would have it, my name was one of three drawn from a raffle bowl, and I was called down to the pitcher's mound along with two other boys to receive an autographed baseball from the great Bob Feller himself. A sports reporter from the old *News Call Bulletin* took a photograph of the winners for the evening newspaper. I was the only boy in the picture without his father.

In his letter Hank said, "You keep seeing them coming and going, and there are all those screams, and then it vanishes." He ended his letter by saying, "I think that Ezra Pound played a better game, even though he denied it in the end. I think he realized he played it a little fancy and too heavy, but he had the guts to admit it."

Gone were those childhood days when I bounced tennis balls off the concrete wall outside our flat on Page Street; living and breathing baseball, playing in pickup games whenever I had the opportunity. San Francisco was a baseball town. There was always a ballgame being played at Big Rec in Golden Gate Park or on various sandlots sponsored by Horse Trader Ed (a used car dealer) or Lucky Lager Beer.

Joe Sprinz was the heart of the Seals. A former catcher whose career ended prematurely when, as part of a publicity stunt for the opening of the Treasure Island World's Fair, he agreed to catch a baseball dropped from an airplane by the immortal Walter Mails.

The ball hit the ground, bounced up, and shattered Sprinz's jaw. He would never again be the same man, never realize his dream of playing Major League baseball. The last I heard he was employed as a doorman at local sporting events.

While stationed in Panama, I played the outfield for the Albrook Flyers baseball team. I played good defense, but my hitting wouldn't have gotten me further than Class A ball. My dream of becoming a baseball player ended the day I tore up my leg trying to stretch a double into a triple during an exhibition game. Like Hank, I knew that those days were long behind me.

At the time of Hank's letter, he was getting over the effects of a television documentary ("Bukowski") produced by a non-profit station. There is little doubt the documentary helped gain his first taste of fame.

In a subsequent letter, Hank said: "I, shit yes, look forward to your special Buk edition, and with that maybe I can get back to the holy grind (poetry)."

He ended his letter by saying, "You seem on the right track. Beware of the bloodsuckers, beware of the friends, beware of the poets, even me."

In November 1973, Hank wrote and said: "Shit, man, I keep telling you to lay off the juices and here I am drunk again. The problem of wandering the streets at night is mainly the cops, but also others out there to get you too. Pressure, you can't breathe free, and then you don't remember much. Sometimes I've really got to think I don't know where I'm at and I'm lucky I've got a place to lie down."

When I was depressed over my Saint Patrick's Day arrest, Hank wrote and cheered me up:

"I know you are down and out, low on coin, spiritually molested like the rest of us, pissed upon by women, racked by haywire nights and hangover mornings, plus a bad past and no future, little chance but to hang on by the fingernails, work a line or two down on paper and walk the street and breathe the air of this shit life they've put upon us and that we've put upon ourselves, but that doesn't mean that I don't read your act; the simple glory of it, putting out this edition . . . the drag of it and the sacrifice of time and $$$ and energy. You're in the bullring, kid, I see you there and it's charging down. I recognize all this. I just assumed that you knew that I knew."

It was during this same period of time Hank left the *Los Angeles Free Press* for the *Weekly News*. He continued writing columns for his popular "Notes Of A Dirty Old Man," which Ferlinghetti would later reissue as a collection under the City Lights imprint.

Bukowski wrote to tell me: "I am still growing up. There's plenty of asshole and feeling in me, Winans. I am still looking for the light in the dark. Keep a little faith in me. It's getting lighter and lighter and lighter."

In January 1974 I went to the printer and picked up the Special

Charles Bukowski issue of *Second Coming*.

I was more involved in the Bukowski issue than any other. I did the typesetting and layout myself. This was the first time I had been as actively involved in the physical production of the magazine. The issue was pleasing to the eye and touch, and the cover was devastating. I've seen a lot of Bukowski photographs, but the cover of the special Bukowski issue rivals any photo ever taken of Hank. I felt a deep sense of pride after reading the issue cover to cover, not once but twice. That night I sat down and packaged Hank several copies of the issue, which I mailed to him the following morning. I didn't write to tell him the issue was on its way, as I wanted it to come as a surprise.

In a long letter, Hank expressed his opinion of the issue, saying that for the most part the contributors had seen him for real, "battered, battering, punchy, but durable, someone trying to get it on out and get it down."

Hank said "I'm glad that we put some dirt and blood on the carpet." He went on to comment on several of the contributors. He said of Micheline: "God Damn what a romantic hustler. He turned them on high. He sings those lines. He's in rhythm and breaking through. He's half bullshit in person, but that's just cover and bad nerves, and too many nights in a cold alley. Micheline knows he has more than 90% of those who have broken through, and it hurts that he hasn't." I understood how Hank felt about Micheline. I had just published a strong political poem of his in *Second Coming*.

I recall even today the way he read his work at the Northeast Mental Health Center and the awe on the faces of the patients who hung on his every word. After the reading I returned home and wrote my first poem for Micheline.

For Jack Micheline

**this poem is for you
and the streets you have walked
from San Francisco to New York
and back again
you who have traveled
the unmarked grave that stretches**

like a long line of coffins
floating the sewers of America
heading East and West where
poets who never had a chance
grasped for Kerouac's dream
buried beneath an ocean of tears
where stone faced politicians
suck the bones to the marrow
feeding on the scraps of the
poor boy poet who like you
carries his vision like
diamonds in the sky

In his letter to me, Hank spoke about Harold Norse simply not being able to see things the way they were:
"Hal was flopping around Switzerland supported by a Contessa, and working on verse while I had blood running down my neck from toting dead steers just slaughtered. Now he's bitter. He shouldn't be. I would have bowed to the Contessa too."

I tried to picture Hank carting those dead steers on his back or carrying them in his beefy arms. Did he wear a bloodstained white apron? Was sweat dripping down his brow? Was the stink of death in the air and permeating his skin? As a teenager I had visited the slaughterhouses in old Butcher Town, and the odor of blood and dead carcasses had stayed with me for days. I had to feel it had stayed with Hank for as long or longer.

Hank admitted that, like the rest of us, he could be an "asshole," and often was. He said when he was drunk he generally was "rude and stupid" like most other drunks. I knew too well what he meant, having played the town drunk in North Beach bars and getting sucker punched more than once by cowardly patrons sensing an easy mark. Hank said if Hal could understand this simple truth, they could still be friends. In his own words, "Before a man can meet the Gods he must learn to forgive the drunks." Hank felt that Alta, editor and publisher of *Shameless Hussy,* suffered from a feminist viewpoint.

"I don't want to rape Alta. I never have, but if the artist wants to go into the mind of a rapist or a murderer and look out that mind and write down that mind, I don't think that's criminal."

Hank was referring to a short story he had written involving the rape of a woman, which Alta found demeaning. I knew how Hank felt. I had published a short story by Jack Micheline that a feminist group found offensive, later defacing several copies of the *Second Coming* issue it appeared in. The irony is that the vandalism took place at City Lights Bookstore where the fight against censorship of *Howl* had been fought. The vandalism upset me, for *Second Coming* was noted for its support of women writers and political causes.

Hank felt Gerald Locklin was accurate in his assessment. He said Locklin was different from the rest of the academic crowd, having learned to write by reading Bukowski. I published several of Locklin's poems over the years I edited and published *Second Coming*, and we corresponded in those early years. It was Locklin who arranged readings for Hank at Long Beach State College, where Locklin worked as an English teacher.

In the special Bukowski issue, Locklin said, "The last time we had him [Bukowski] down for readings at Long Beach, he was truly a pain in the ass. The noon reading was no problem - we'd only had time for a few beers on the way - but we went to the Forty-Niner Tavern for the afternoon, where by four o'clock Bukowski the good had become his unruly, rude, bullying-styled demented genius." Locklin said by the time of the evening reading "Bukowski could hardly talk, let alone discern many of the words on the page." According to Locklin, Hank alternately encouraged and insulted questioners, rocking back and forth upon the podium like a "surreal caricature of George Putnam."

"I sat back, laughing in spite of myself, while reeling off rosaries that he might not topple from the stage and break his neck. The reading was supposed to last for two hours, but ended in one." Locklin felt Bukowski had given the audience what they had paid for, and that they got a bonus when Bukowski accompanied Locklin and some of the students for more drinking at the "Niner" tavern.

This would be pretty much the pattern, except Hank normally stayed just sober enough to be able to give the full reading. After the fabled reading, Hank and Locklin became close friends, as close as one could get to Hank.

Hank was critical of Linda King's essay, which went into intimate details of their relationship. I believe Hank felt uncomfortable about some of her revelations. He said Linda came off as too defensive and had opted for a "female libber stance."

"I'm afraid her mind stance at the time was just too precious, which means that she failed, just like I do sometimes."

Hank believed that when a female writer moves into "the libber stance" she loses "her juices." He said, "Women's Lib is just like God. It destroys individual thinking."

Hank was neutral on some of the other contributors, but was anything but kind toward Hugh Fox, a small press veteran, who was a Professor of English at Michigan State University. Hank was skeptical that Fox had ever taken a physical beating in his life.

"Getting off your knees in an alley with fourteen drunks watching, and before you can get your hands up to your knees, the other guy lands another blow and gives you a knee in the nuts as you are down and out; nothing to do but get up, until finally it becomes a matter of breathing. You can hardly breathe and neither can the man who is murdering you. And finally, when you start to come back on him, the crowd steps in and stops the fight. You get into seven or nine of these things and you know what a physical beating is."

Hank may have been describing the fight scene in the alley from his movie *Barfly*. To this day, I'm not sure why Hank felt the way he did about Fox. Fox was writing for the small presses long before Locklin, and hardly represents the academic mode of writing.

Hank liked what Santa Monica poet and painter Steve Richmond had to say about him. He felt it was best for Richmond to remain unknown. He reasoned, "a man has to have time to build walls so that if he is finally discovered he will be able to go on."

Hank said, "I like Richmond. He knows how to give due to the object without destroying the object involved. This is no easy thing. He also knows how to write a sentence."

It wasn't always this rosy. In the Spring 1974 issue of Norse's *Bastard Angel,* Norse charged Hank with bullying people into submission. He cited the mutual adoration between Richmond and Hank in the Bukowski *Second Coming* issue. Backing his claim, Norse published a letter by Richmond that had earlier been published in the *Holy Doors* anthology. Richmond said:

"The lie . . . is in saying that I somehow pushed my poems on Bukowski when he came over here and yelled at me to see them. Get me the poems. Get me the poems. I need them for *Laugh Lit* [a small magazine Hank co-produced with Neeli Cherry].

"Then I read his fucking poem called '300 Poems,' in his new book. What a disappointment. The lie in art. He [Buk] calls it art form. I call it bullshit. I see it as duplicity and told the old man to keep away from here for good. That's my particular hassle with Bukowski . . . his limitation is his imposition or attempted imposition of his own ideas of living on others.

"That's why all faces look dead and wooden to him, and that's why his work will be forgotten in fifty years."

Bukowski responded by saying Richmond was untalented. "I only ask that you measure the totality of my work against theirs (his detractors). I'm afraid that the small presses, the mimeo presses, have kept alive too many talentless darlings and have made it difficult for their wives, their children, and their girlfriends. Let time itself answer the attacks on me by Richmond and Fox. As for me, I've wasted enough time on them. Oh, my little friends, how you cry and weep and bawl and puke and slobber over yourselves. May I suggest that you use more of your energy on what you pretend is your craft (writing). There seems room for improvement. Someday you may be men."

This was the dark side of Bukowski that Norse spoke about in his poem. Hank could be cruel and vicious, whether it was warranted or not.

Contrast this with a 1982 letter Bukowski wrote Richmond, in which Hank said:

"You've been the most overlooked talent I can think of. You've put up a good fight down there. You've held the stance. Another test will come when the fame comes, but I think you can beat that too."

These two letters show how Hank discarded friends, only to later bring them back into his good graces. However, most people once discarded were gone for good.

But back to Norse. To further his point, Norse related that before the bad exchange between Richmond and Hank, Hank had written a foreword for Richmond's second collection of poems, highly praising Richmond and his work. Norse felt that Hank could dish it out far better than he could take it. He pointed out that Richmond completely reversed himself in his essay in the *Second Coming* Bukowski issue:

"We all back stab each other to reach false heights. Those who have felt knifed by Bukowski have to admit that he has penetrated their own souls and fittingly described the mess within."

In Richmond's book *Spinning Off Bukowski* he once again heaped praise on Hank, barely touching on their tendency to put each other down over the years.

Hank remained strangely silent about his one-time close friend Neeli Cherry (Cherkovski), who contributed a piece detailing his experiences with Hank when they had been close drinking companions in the days before Hank became famous. Neeli often visited Hank in those early days: "Drinking, taking bennies, smoking grass, dropping acid, and taking wild drives through Hollywood at two in the morning." It was not until much later that Hank became a loner.

When all was said and done, Hank felt the *Second Coming* Bukowski issue was a success. He believed, however, that some of the contributors had picked up a certain style and meaning in his life:

"I never mean my way to be their way. They can have theirs, and I don't think that they can fit into mine. That's fair. I do much of my stuff out of tune, out of one ear. We don't want a mythology here. It was just a way to go, and there's still tomorrow."

Ten

With the Bukowski issue behind me, I turned my attention to publishing William Wantling's poetry chapbook (*7 On Style*). Wantling spent several years in San Quentin for armed robbery. Along with Gene Fowler, another San Quentin graduate, Wantling quickly gained recognition as a member of the "Meat" school of poetry.

He was one of several prison poets *Second Coming* published. Other prison poets included Gene Fowler, Ed Lipman and Pancho Aguila.

Micheline and I frequently participated in the Folsom Prison Writer's Workshop. I remember all too well my first visit there. I pulled my car into the parking lot and shared a half-pint of vodka with Micheline before we made our way to the prison gates. Once inside, we were led into a waiting room, where we were made to empty our pockets and pass through a metal detector. We weren't allowed to take anything inside except our poems and notebooks, not even a pack of Rolaids, which I was forced to surrender to a stern-looking guard. We were escorted into the courtyard and taken to a small room. A group of about fifteen prisoners was waiting for our arrival, sitting around a large table. A few of the prisoners were there for no other reason than to pass the time. But the majority of the participants were poets, or at least interested in poetry. Micheline read first and was greeted with warm applause. When it came my turn to read, I saw several of the men intently staring at me from behind dark sunglasses. I could feel their eyes boring into me like a laser beam.

I started by reading my long "America Poem" which quickly won them over, and finished with several "street" poems, poems about the homeless, the junkies, the whores, and the downtrodden souls of America. At the close of the workshop I invited the men to submit their work to *Second Coming* for consideration.

At the end of the day Ross Lawson, Chairman of the workshop, showed me a letter he had written inviting Ferlinghetti to visit the workshop as a guest poet. Lawson and the other workshop writers were disappointed because Ferlinghetti had failed to respond to their request.

I later ran into Ferlinghetti at the Cafe Trieste and told him that the prison writers were upset that he had ignored their invitation.

Ferlinghetti was sitting with a group of young writers, and I recall his smiling and telling me he had never received such an invitation.

"It must be a figment of their imagination," Ferlinghetti said, but I knew differently. The old revolutionary had copped out. The incident brought back memories of Shig Murao, the former manager of City Lights (and long-time friend of Ferlinghetti), who suffered a bad stroke. Following a recovery period Shig returned to City Lights to assume his former duties, only to learn that Ferlinghetti had replaced him with a younger and more business-minded manager.

Whenever asked about the situation, Shig would smile and reply, "You mean Mr. Spaghetti."

After returning home from my first visit to the Folsom Prison Writer's Workshop, I sat down and wrote a poem entitled "Visiting Folsom Prison."

Visiting Folsom Prison

The guards joke and laugh
As they have me empty my pockets
Inside out
Taking everything from me
Even a pack of unopened
Rolaids
Perhaps in fear they
Might be coated with
LSD
Leaving me with only
My notebook
And a handful of poems

The guard in the watch tower
Watches the prisoners in
The court yard below

His hi-powered rifle
At the ready
The warden distrustful
Maybe even fearful
Stations a guard inside
The small room where
The Poetry workshop
Is held.

The sharing of words
Barely begins when
I look outside the window
And see a bird light
On top of the prison wall
Looking East then
West before spreading
Its wings and flying
North
Free as free was meant
To be
As I turn my attention
To the guard in
The back of the room
Hiding behind dark shades
Looking more the outlaw than
The law

I never had the privilege of meeting Wantling in person. I first became familiar with his work after reading Len Fulton's *Dust* magazine and Hugh Fox's *Living Underground Anthology.* Wantling and I soon began a semi-regular correspondence, and I later published some of his poetry in early issues of *Second Coming.* Wantling had a long-standing fight with drugs. In his own words:

"When I was in Korea, they gave me my first shot of morphine. It killed the pain. It was beautiful. Five years later I was in San Quentin on narcotics."

Len Fulton has described Wantling as "a man of huge contrasts, a wrestler's physique, a Keatsian sensitivity and a genius reach. A poet with rich images and intensity." I found Wantling to be all this and more. At his best, he could hold his own with Bukowski and others who practiced their trade in the 60's and early 70's. I quote from Wantling's poem "Heroin":

> **And once, high**
> **so high I never reached that peak**
> **again, happy my wife & I**
> **lie coasting beside a small pond**
> **in an impossibly green park**
> **under a god blue sky**
> **birds swimming V's on the smoky water**
> **the sun weaving patterns through the**
> **leaves, small shadows swimming on**
> **her face & arms**
> **& she says - Baby, I feel so fine**
> **so fine...**
> **that was twice**
> **the rest was nothing, even**
> **less**
> **the pain's still there**

Wantling was going through some hard times when we began corresponding. I wanted to lift his spirits and decided to re-publish some of his poems from the old days. When I learned he had completed a small book of poems (*7 On Style),* I asked him if I could look at it. I knew he was trying hard to stay straight, as evidenced in another poem:

> **goodbye Fix on Saturday night**
> **when Fat Mama slips me a dime**
> **goodbye long lemon & white port swill**
> **for the bone-ache days ahead & behind**
> **& goodbye white man's god**
> **& goodbye that Fool Allah too**
> **it's always Power they wants**
> **& they steal that Power from you**

I wrote Wantling and included a short poem I had written after watching a friend shoot up in a housing project:

> **burned spoon hovering over**
> **hot flame**
> **like a moth drawn**
> **to a light bulb**
> **arm stretched tight**
> **with rubber tubing**
> **liquid death riding**
> **near invisible vein**
>
> **eyes closed dream**
> **like**
> **resembling a cowboy**
> **looking forward**
> **to the next trail**
> **drive.**

Shortly afterwards, he wrote telling me how much he liked the poem, and included his manuscript *7 On Style*. It took one reading for me to know I wanted to publish it, and Wantling seemed excited about the prospect. During the production of the book I received a long letter from Wantling. I've since reread the letter many times, and can now see subtle hints of a man walking on a narrow window ledge, afraid to look down.

I had heard through the grapevine that Wantling was feeling the dark underbelly of depression, and I wanted to let him know I too was no stranger to this terrible beast. I sent him a poem about an earlier bout I had experienced with depression:

Depression

It's as if the weight of Buddha
is sitting on my shoulders
It's as if Jesus were pressing
His cold purple lips to mine
It's as if the Virgin Mary
Is drowning me in tears
It's as if God were holding
Judgment day inside
My head
It's as if day and night
Were one
It's as if the clock is stuck
At half-past dead
It's as if the holy ghost
Is riding through my brain
On a pair of snow shoes
It's as if a hammer
Is pounding at my heart

It's as if my every thought
Is lost between the legs
Of a cosmic whore
It's as if I am riding the
Coat tails of Haley's comet

Wantling wrote back to tell me how much he liked the poem. "Good to get your letter. Any little bit of encouragement helps at this point, if it's honest. Rough yellow brick road ahead right now. Got a shrink to write me a prescription for uppers, and try my best to keep off the juice. But now I abuse the uppers, and being nervous to begin with, I'd almost settle for the juice again.

"I spend the long evenings alone in my bachelor's crash pad, having broken up with Ruthie [his wife], humming like an over-loaded high line, trying my damnedest to write, but instead fooling around with nuts and bolts. You know, building things. Don't ask me what. Fumbling with shiny gadgets and jacking-off in the lonely dark. Not writing because I'm lost in my mind again. Don't know where I'm at or even if it's important."

I told him I could no longer handle hard liquor and informed him about my second DUI arrest. The arrest earned me a trip to the Oakland drunk tank, where I was introduced with no fanfare to the sharp end of a Deputy Sheriff's nightstick. Wantling wrote back and said that when arrested, a person needed to learn to keep his mouth shut. "It doesn't pay to say anything more than 'yes sir' and that even this could get you in trouble." He responded to comments I made about drugs.

"It's a medical fact that it's far better to use smack, if use something you must. Sometimes I can cool it for months on just beer and grass, but it runs in cycles. Suicide. A binge drinker. I drink nothing for months and there's no problem. Then the old snake which coils down the solar plexus, and which if you work it right, and with discipline, can be the powerful Kundalini of Yoga fame, but which is (with cats like you and me) our death waiting like runaway cancer to strike.

"I want to go out sideways, but pain hurts. It scares me to think of even a bullet in the brain because there's that unbelievable pain which, only microseconds long as we count it, can be a subjective eternity burning in napalm."

Alcohol, drugs, insanity! My second drunk driving arrest began in North Beach, and again it was my old nemesis, Jack Daniels. All I recall is trying to drive home but somehow winding up on the Bay Bridge. Here I was on the bridge, headed for God only knows where, when I heard what I thought were voices coming from inside my head. I couldn't make out what the voices were saying. I became aware of flashing red lights in my rear view mirror as the voices grew louder. This time they were painfully clear to me.

"Pull over to the side of the road and turn your engine off. This is the Highway Patrol. Pull over to the side of the road and remain in your car. I repeat, pull over to the side of the road and turn your engine off. Remain inside of your car."

I realized the officers were addressing me through a police bull-horn. The rest was anti-climatic. I was told to get out of the car. I was frisked, handcuffed, and put in the back seat of the Highway Patrol car, and driven to the downtown Oakland Jail.

The Highway Patrol officers were different from the San Francisco

Police. They were polite and professional. One of the officers even drove my car off the freeway and parked it near the police station, saving me an expensive towing bill. I was given a blood alcohol test and put in a drunk tank by myself. I don't remember what the legal limit was in those days but I was well over it.

In my letter to Wantling I discussed his weakness for drugs compared to my own weakness for alcohol. Wantling told me he had once overdosed on "smack," and vividly recalled the horror of the moment when he realized there was no turning back.

Several of his friends saved his life, which was astonishing since his OD was the result of his having "burned" these same friends for their share of the stash. He said from that day on he made a conscious decision to take the easy way out and filled his room with bottles of booze. On waking up, finding one bottle and then another, he drank until sleep finally came:

"I just wanted to sleep and never return to the real world. I would lie in the corner with vomit on me and ask to be left alone, but they never would. You know, you named it, suicide. Only it was a half-assed suicide, just like everything else that I do except poetry." Wantling closed his letter with some advice: "Do that prose you talk about doing. Fuck the magazine. Be selfish with your talent, not your life. Good advice from someone who can't follow it himself."

Shortly after I received his letter he died from a combination overdose of alcohol and drugs, purchased for him by a young student in one of his classes at Illinois State University.

I wrote Hank and asked if he would be interested in writing a foreword for Wantling's book *7 On Style.* He wrote back and said:

"I picked up on Bill all the way. So, sure I'd like to do the foreword to *Style.* Wantling had been sending me some of the *Style* poems, but I can't seem to locate them. If I do a foreword, of course, I'd like to see the poems." Hank told me Wantling had offered him a few pills of some kind or another when Hank visited Illinois State University to give a reading. Hank declined, having quit taking pills of any kind for a long time.

Hank told me he was busy working on a second novel and said: "Whenever I don't answer a letter to you right off, understand that I am fucked up in one way or another, but when and if I pull through you'll hear from me." That night and into the early morning hours I wrote a poem for Wantling:

Linda King and Charles Bukowski, Phoenix, AZ 1973

With Bob Kaufman, Cafe Trieste, North Beach, San Francisco 1977. *Photo by Richard Morris*

Bob Kaufman and Harold Norse at a party celebrating publication of Second Coming Press *California Poets Anthology*, San Francisco 1976. *Photo by J. Whitebird*

Neeli Cherkovski
at Corso Memorial Reading
New College of California,
San Francisco 2001
Photo by A.D. Winans

Lawrence Ferlinghetti
City Lights Bookstore
San Francisco 2000

Photo by A.D. Winans

Poster in
window of
City Lights
Bookstore
on Kerouac
Alley, San
Francisco
2001

*Photo by
A.D. Winans*

With Bobby Kennedy, Washington, DC 1966

**With Alix Geluardi in courtyard at annual
Spec's Bar Party, North Beach 1970's**
Photo by Mark Green

With Jack Micheline outside Books Plus following Second Coming Book Reading, San Francisco 1976
Photo by Joel Deutch

With Ed "Foots" Lipman at the home of Bil Paul, celebrating publication of *Second Coming California Poets Anthology*, San Francisco 1976
Photo by Bil Paul

With poet Joanie
Whitebird outside
my Laidley Street
Apartment
San Francisco 1976

**Presenting Music Achievement Award to the late John Lee
Hooker at California Polk Hall at Second Coming 1980 Poets
and Music Festival.** *Photo by Wilfredo Castano*

With George Tsongas and Kell Robertson. Vesuvio Bar, San Francisco 2000. *Photo by Annie Menebroker*

With Arthur Knight at memorial for poet Paul Mariah 1990's

Photo by Kit Knight

The late Illinois
poet William
Wantling
Circa 1973

**Charles Bukowski
1994**

*Compliments of
Al Berlinsky*

Jan Kerouac

Photo by Gerald Nicosia

Neeli Cherkovski and Harold Norse, City Lights Bookstore 1979
Photo by Raymond Foye

Diane Comen
and
Hugh Fox
1980 NYC
COSMEP
Conference
1980

*Photo by
Richard Morris*

**With Paul Fericano, 1978 Night of Street Poetry Reading
San Francisco.** *Photo by Roger Langton*

Gerald Nicosia
Corso Memorial
Reading
San Francisco
2001

Photo by A.D. Winans

Michael McClure, Corso Memorial Reading, San Francisco 2001
Photo by A.D. Winans

Night of Street Poetry Reading
Neighborhood Arts Theater,
University of California
Extension Center,
San Francisco 1978

Photo by Roger Langton

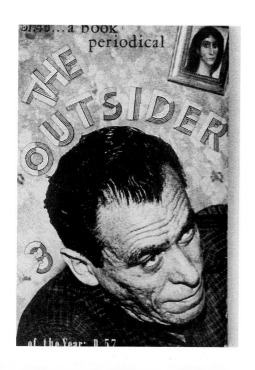

Charles Bukowski on cover
of *The Outsider* edited
by Jon and Gypsy Lou Webb
1971

**With Richard Morris (COSMEP) and Len Fulton (Dustbooks)
San Francisco 1977**

**Leonard Randolph (National Endowment Literature Director)
and Len Fulton (Dustbooks), Portland, Oregon 1976**

With Paddy O'Sullivan outside Cafe Trieste, San Francisco 1977
photo by Richard Morris

With Richard Morris at COSMEP Conference, NYC 1980
Photo by Hugh Fox

**With Kit Knight,
San Francisco
1998**

*Photo by
Arthur Knight*

Looking into the cracked lips of sorrow
I walk the harsh streets of tomorrow
The ghost of my fears
Demanding that I face my destiny
But I am not a graveyard poet
In search of chilled bones
The words I speak
Hold no fear
For like you
I have tasted
The laughter of life
Walked the sinister circus
Of reality
Playing out the game
Like a chess master
Knowing there is no power
Strong enough to still
The song inside you.

The long years of silence
The grave brings can only
Be broken by those who care
Enough to take up the cause

There are those who seek
The underground warmth
Desire to be closeted in blackness
Moths of night with closed minds
And hardened hearts encased in stone
And then there are those like you
Who know that to be a poet
One must first die
For inspiration comes naturally
But expiration takes effort
The night rolling back its wings
With teeth cold as naked bone
But neither the night
Or the poet dies quietly

Only the flesh expires
The words linger on welcoming
The taste of ash.

And morning comes as no loss
For wherever you are
You survived the pain
Refused to surrender
Earth's flesh removed
From reality
Here in the early hours
Of dawn where
The mist smells sweetly
And no one can hear
The throats of birds singing
Like cannons
In the hour when the spirit
Collects its visions replaying
Them on old walls
Gatsby shorts from another era
Stills that fill the void
In a world of runaway tongues

You are everywhere beneath
The wild grass
Riding the silver star of night
The crystal sky singing
Your song
Gone with other poets
Who dared to kiss
The sun

I mailed the poem to Hank, and shortly afterwards he wrote back and said he thought it was a fitting tribute to Wantling. He told me how impressed he had been with Wantling on their first meeting. This is best expressed in a letter Hank wrote to Trevor Reeves of *Cave Magazine* before Wantling's death.

"I saw Wantling, babe. He's a holy man. A human, human."

Hank went on to say that Ruthie (Wantling's wife) had called to tell him Wantling had died. In his letter, he said: "Wantling worked the art-form well, but the other form was there too . . . somebody sitting in a chair, lighting a cigarette, being warm and easy and exactly what he is without the con or balderdash or bullshit that so many have that pretend at truth and at art and at entertainment or at anything enlightening. Wantling was a man, a human and an artist; we all die, that's no big trick, but I felt his easy rays and yet his straight acceptance of factuality. I met him; I then came back, got fucked up with the horses, drinking, arguments with a woman, my own weak madness. I meant to write him a letter and did. I told him, you have style, you have the ultimate style. I doubt that the letter got to him. I waited too long. But meeting him taught me that you can't be automatically disgusted with all men; there is always hope, there is always a Wantling somewhere, in Illinois, in Hong Kong, under the ground or at a railway station. The miracle never quits; therefore we must not until it finally closes in."

Trevor and I became friends in the early 70's. First as a poet contributing to *Cave Magazine*, and later as the U.S. distributor for Wantling's *San Quentin Stranger,* published by Cave Press. He and I worked together to try and bridge the gap between poetry in the U.S. and New Zealand, which culminated with my publishing a special New Zealand poetry anthology. Trevor later wrote and said the New Zealand anthology helped expand the narrow styles that existed with New Zealand writers at the time.

At the time there existed a Bukowski cult in New Zealand, much of it centered around Cave Press. Wantling and Bukowski were the leaders of the cult, and remain legends among many today.

Walter Lowenfels (who died a few years later) wrote, saying, "Wantling used words as bullets that crack open what he felt and had to be said. There is terrible experience in much of his best work: war, jail, drugs and no salvation except *Style*, how you transform your terror into a poem."

And the terror was all too real for Wantling, as expressed in many of the poems in his book *San Quentin Stranger.* I quote from a poem titled "Poetry":

**the other day I was walking
in the lower exercise yard here
at San Quentin and this cat called
Turk came up to a friend of mine
and said Ernie, I hear You're
shooting on my kid. And Ernie
told him so what, Punk? And Turk
pulled out his stuff and shanked
Ernie in the gut only Ernie had a
metal tray in his shirt. Turk's
shank bounced off Ernie and
Ernie pulled his stuff out and of
course Turk didn't have a tray and
he caught it dead in the chest, a bad
one and the blood that came to his
lips was a bright pink, lung blood
and he just laid down in the grass
and said Shit. Fuck it. Sheeit.**

Wantling said he could make good word music and rhyme at the right times, fit words together to give people pleasure, and even sometimes take their breath away, but it seemed phony. Consonance and assonance and inner rhyme could not make up for the fact that he couldn't figure out how to get down on paper the real or the true or this thing called life. Wantling conveyed this feeling in the last two stanzas of his poem.

**Fuck it. And he laughed a soft long
laugh, 5 minutes then died. Now
what could consonance or assonance or
even rhyme do with something like that?**

This is what I believe drew Wantling to Hank. Wantling lived life to the fullest and wrote about it in a direct and honest manner.

Hank began his foreword for *7 On Style* about the same time Ruthie

100

Wantling wrote and asked me to use a foreword by Walter Lowenfels, and enclosed a copy of it for me to look at.

Lowenfels and Wantling had been close friends, but I sensed there was something amiss between Ruthie and Hank. It made me think back to John Bryan and how he ended his relationship with Hank after Hank allegedly tried to put the make on Bryan's wife. Did Hank try the same thing with Ruthie? One can only wonder. In his novel *Women*, there are sections in the book which indicate he may have done this. This despite Hank's July 1974 letter to his friend and German translator, Carl Weissner, indicating otherwise.

In Hank's novel *Women,* Ruthie appears under a fictitious name and is characterized as telling Hank she was coming to San Francisco to discuss Wantling's book manuscript with me, which was not true. There was never any telephone conversation between Ruthie and me. Our relationship was entirely through the mail. In his letter to Weissner, Bukowski said: "Supposed to write a foreword to one of Wantling's last books [*Style*]. I did but his old lady came here and we didn't make it at all - total opposites."

Hank informed Weissner that Ruthie would probably nix the foreword, but the truth is Ruthie had no control over it. The decision was mine alone to make, and I at no time consulted her about it. These discrepancies make me wonder how much reality there is to Hank's supposedly biographical novel *Women.*

Hank's foreword arrived a few days after Ruthie's letter. I read both forewords several times and decided to go with the shorter Lowenfels foreword. It addressed Wantling's work while Hank's foreword was more Bukowski than Wantling. When I told Hank I was considering Lowenfels' foreword, he wrote back and said:

"If it doesn't work for you then send it back. That's what editors are for, for making decisions."

While working on the production of *7 On Style,* I heard from Hank again. He informed me he was alone again and he was trying out different women.

"As long as the women don't stay for more than a night or two, things work out well enough," he said. He went on to say he was working on his new novel and life was putting him through the wringer.

"What a forest we have to hack through. What a drag. What a limp moon. What a dirty dog ass rubbed in the grass of ants and the worms and Aunt Jemima."

I had earlier mailed Hank a check for $25 as a small payment for some of his work I had used in *Second Coming*. Hank thanked me for the check, and talked about how $25 might not seem like much money to most people, but that it meant a lot when one was approaching the end of the month and down to his last dollar. I was still feeling a certain degree of guilt about asking him to do the Wantling foreword and later rejecting it. Hank wrote and said: "In this game, we all get stuff back, and sometimes stuff gets published that would have been better tossed out with the used condoms."

Eleven

I sent Hank a copy of my special *Second Coming* New Zealand anthology, knowing he had corresponded with Trevor Reeves and that he might find it interesting. In return Hank sent a past issue of *Cave Magazine* which contained some of his poems and his photo on the front cover. Hank had just returned from giving a series of readings and said: "Been on the reading kick . . . the old survival suck . . . Detroit, Riverside, Santa Cruz."

He read in Santa Cruz with Ferlinghetti and Ginsberg and had drawn 1600 people at three dollars a head. The reading was a benefit for Americans in Mexican jails "after the poets got their bit of cream." Hank said:

"There was a bomb threat and old Alan's ears jumped. He got on stage and improvised a poem about the situation. Ginsberg was all right, he seemed a good sort."

In a later telephone conversation he talked at length about the early days when he and Neeli Cherry (Cherkovski) had co-edited *Laugh Literary And Man The Humping Guns*. Hank said the poetry submissions were so bad that he and Neeli had been forced to publish their own work under pseudonyms. Hank felt badly about a letter he had sent Wantling after rejecting some of his poems, and quoted from one of the rejection slips:

"I've seen better from you, and your work was never that good to begin with. Get with it fucker, and next time don't include a self-addressed, stamped envelope that is glued together at both ends." Hank expressed remorse that Wantling might have taken the letter seriously instead of seeing it in the "humorous vein" it was meant to be.

Hank and Neeli began editing and publishing *Laugh Literary* in 1969, long before Hank became famous. The magazine lasted only three issues, ceasing publication in 1972. The magazine was never a serious literary publication, but more of a self-serving vehicle for Hank and Neeli . . . a kind of self-indulgent funny-bone trip. Neither Hank nor Neeli made an effort to hide their contempt for the poets who submitted their work. This is confirmed in a letter from Hank to Richard Morris in 1972. Morris was putting together a literary newsletter and was seeking viewpoints from established writers on the state of small press publishing. Hank responded to Morris' inquiry by saying:

"All right, I'll do something on the little mag 'impotency' scene if it comes to my mind naturally. Yes, I get the littles in the mail and the little mag poet books and, god, I've learned to toss them. They land on the floor.

"I know there's nothing; it's time tested forever. I remember one night Neeli Cherry and I reading submissions to *Laugh.* They had stacked up. The lack of talent was miraculous. It was so bad that we began laughing and rolling on the floor. Finally pissed on the manuscripts, poured beer on them, burned them and mailed the remains back. Not kind but Jesus it was a release."

In early 1975 a documentary film on Hank's life was premiered at the Whitney museum, along with a film on the life of Henry Miller. The film received a favorable review in the *New York Times,* and Hank was on his way to stardom.

In late February 1975, I wrote Hank and told him the California Arts Council was providing me with grant support for the publication of a *Second Coming* California bicentennial poetry anthology. I invited him to send some poems for consideration. Hank sent several poems and said he felt honored to be part of the anthology, which would ultimately turn out to be the most financially successful *Second Coming* publication.

Rumors are common in the literary world, so I was not surprised when Hank wrote and said, "Word is leaking out down here that you're getting drunk up there and kicking ass. The way I look at it, Friscowise, is that any ass you kick is the right one."

Hank had just finished his second novel *Factotum* and Black Sparrow planned on publishing it early in the fall. It came out on schedule, a factual book on Bukowski presented as fiction. The book shows Hank going from one dreary job to another, along the way working in warehouses, cleaning toilets, and unloading trucks, all back breaking or de-humanizing jobs. The reader is treated to a generous sampling of Hank's humor in the form of crazy bosses and fellow co-workers. Hank comes off as a Walter Mitty character going from job to job, defying the odds, but always managing to maintain his spirit and sanity.

Hank told me he felt his work was becoming a bit thin by writing poetry, short stories and a novel all at the same time. He felt it would be a long time before he could focus on the "man/woman situation," which he described as "a big bite out of the lurking dark." He brought up my past visit to Linda King's home, and told me RB had later called him and tried to arrange an interview. Hank said:

"I cursed him right off the telephone. I've got good instincts. This guy is pure grade A poison, more enemy to anything close to a possible good than anybody I've met in years. Parts of him run up and down the walls like roaches. Some men are natural enemies. I never try to be kind when I know that kindness will be wasted."

Hank was accurate in his assessment of RB, whom I had met through Charles Price (Cheap Charley as he was known in North Beach). RB worked as an assistant editor for one of the men's magazines, but was a frustrated poet at heart. It wasn't until after my visit with Hank that I learned RB was seriously involved with drugs. Hank ended his letter by saying I should drink alone and keep it down to beer; that there was nothing on the streets - men or women, let alone poets.

By early 1976 Hank was making notes for his third novel, *Women.* Two years later the book saw print. Shortly afterwards the *California Poets Anthology* was published. The anthology not only contained Bukowski, but work from every conceivable school of poetry.

Neeli Cherkovski would later write and say *Second Coming* was multi-cultural long before the term became fashionable. A review in *Library Journal* brought in several hundred orders from libraries nationwide.

It was around this time I began experiencing severe abdominal pain and thought I might have an ulcer. My worst fear was the pain might be a sign of stomach cancer. I began having trouble keeping food down. When I expressed my concern to Hank, he wrote back and said, "Spit your stomach out and forget it. Hospitals have become billing factories, flown doves and shrimp assholes." Hank said he had given a reading for a thousand dollars, the most money he had ever received for a performance. He said in the future his minimum reading fee would be $500 plus expenses.

Shortly afterwards I wrote and asked him if he would write an introduction for my latest book of poetry, *North Beach Poems.* I was disappointed when he begged off:

"I can't do any more introductions. I've done too many of them. All these guys later do is show up at some chick's place where I have given up on her, and want to fuck her, and maybe do. That's all right, but somehow the whole symphony lacks a grace that I wished was there, somewhere."

I found his response puzzling to say the least. Hadn't he told me "Kid, you keep your ass in Northern California and leave Southern California to me?" The ironic part is I had just returned home from a series of readings in Los Angeles. The *Los Angeles Times* had announced my arrival and I was met at the airport and whisked away for an interview at a local radio station.

Hank had just returned home from Europe during the last two days of my Los Angeles trip. He told me to make sure to call him if I was ever in the area. But when I called him he seemed aloof. He said he was tired from his trip to Europe and couldn't see me. I was hurt at what I considered a snub, and later wrote a poem about the incident.

Thanks A Lot Hank

called you from the corner
of Hollywood and Vine
because you said to be sure
and look you up when
I got in town
managed to reach you
late in the afternoon
on the night of my reading
at Beyond Baroque
and you said
you had trouble recognizing
my voice
and hoped I wasn't drinking
too much
said something about
your having just returned
from Europe with Linda

3 weeks of intense travel
3 weeks of hell
and an appearance
on national television
said that I had called
at the wrong time
and hoped that I understood
and to be sure and write
when I got back home
and me just back from
8 days and nights fighting
insomnia in New York
listening to Louis Simpson
and a host of minor poets
here in Los Angeles
3 days into smog
3 nights into
the World Series
don't worry Hank
I understand
don't give it a thought
I mean it's okay
we all have a little of the
gangster inside us
Al Capone or
Dillinger.

we all dream
the dream of Diamond Jim
only to wake in the morning
sweating, a dead numbers man
in Chicago or Vegas
or in downtown
L.A.
and the sleepless nights
pile up like litter
and the mafia men
disguised in the clothes

of poets wait like
hit men to collect
a bad debt
and there is always a torpedo
from Cleveland or the Bronx
someone with a scar and a sneer
waiting by the window with
a machine gun
or a forty-five
and if the arts and politics
don't get you
and you somehow manage
to survive the betrayals
and the long line of undertakers
that stretch out like body bags
in a battle zone
you can consider yourself lucky
and sell your letters
to the university
and ignore the mad sirens
wailing in your mind

don't worry Hank
I understand
like Bob Kaufman said
"there ain't no piano
for Lucky Luciano
there ain't no phone
for Al Capone

there ain't no jazz
on Alcatraz
there ain't no heart
on Carleton.

I thought perhaps Hank felt I was invading his turf, but this wasn't the case. It was the first time I had read in the Los Angeles area. It would be twenty-five years before I returned to give another reading.

What disturbed me most about Hank's refusal to write a foreword for *North Beach Poems* was that on more than one occasion he had stated he liked my work. He had no qualms about writing introductions for poets of questionable talent, but found weak excuses to turn me and Jack Micheline down.

In 1973, he responded to Micheline's request to write an introduction to a new book of poems:

"Thanks for sending, but things are happening. I am in a bad mental state, can barely hold the threads together. It's the same thing that has happened to me before, but I can never understand it. The knives are into me, Jack. I can't do the foreword. Bless your balls and hold on." Now here he was years later writing me and begging off for reasons that didn't apply to me. If he didn't like the book, all he had to do was be honest with me. In closing, Hank said:

"I am in trouble with women as usual. They are getting younger and more vicious and more beautiful. They are my superiors. They kill me, almost. Let me Jesus hear from you, Pancho. I think you could go six rounds with the best of them."

Damn! In one breath he was refusing to do a foreword and in the next breath he was telling me I could "go six rounds with the best of them." His refusal hurt and I expressed my feelings to him in a drunken telephone conversation, in which Hank said, "Call me an asshole, call me a prick, and I understand, but I still can't do it." To my surprise, he later sent me a quote to use for the back cover of *North Beach Poems*.

"A. D. Winans is one of the few writers that I have met (and I have met too God Damned many of them) who doesn't *act* like a writer or think of himself continually as a writer, and maybe that's why he writes better than they do. I always prefer a man that I can tolerate for more than ten minutes. That's rare, and so is A. D."

Hank and I continued our correspondence and occasional telephone conversations. I wrote and told him I met a female poet at a publisher's conference in Texas, and we wound up having a brief affair. I related how relaxing it had been to divorce myself from the politics of the literary world, and the freedom of relaxing in the arms of a woman who, at the time, asked for and expected nothing from me. I felt comfortable discussing intimate details with Hank. We often discussed women, and how they related to our lives and art. How a woman can be good for the writing process but at the same time tax your creative efforts with too many personal demands on you. Hank and I were satisfied with drinking, listening to music and going to the racetrack.

The Texas woman (JW) and I began a brief affair in Austin after she rescued me from a roach-infested college dormitory and put me up at her home. Hank later met JW in San Francisco, where he found himself the subject of intense literary gossip after he paid her round-trip airfare. It appears Hank fell hard for JW and wanted her to visit him in Los Angeles, but she had insisted he meet her in San Francisco. How the airfare was worked out, I don't know. What I do know is the arrangements she made with Hank coincided with her plans to visit me. I would become an unwitting pawn in a plot that could have come straight out of a television soap opera. JW would later write an article for a literary newspaper detailing the events.

At the time I wrote Hank about meeting JW in Texas, I had no idea he had met her earlier at the small Houston museum she worked for. JW had somehow convinced him to give a reading at the museum, and got them to come up with Hank's $500 asking fee.

Twelve

Not long afterwards, the museum was damaged by fire. JW wrote Hank and asked for his help. Hank told me he felt JW was asking him for money.

"For all the *Rolling Stone* [interview with him] bit and whatever, I'm still eligible for food stamps off my royalties which only amount to $300 a month, and I have to pay child support too. Not to cry, but I am crying. It's just not as good as it may seem to some, but it's okay as long as I'm not working a mop across a restroom floor, if you know what I mean." Having worked menial jobs myself, I knew all too well what Hank meant.

When JW got Hank to pay for her airfare to San Francisco, she surely had to have an agenda in mind. I'm not sure just what her intentions were. Had she agreed to meet Hank in San Francisco so he would pay her airfare in order to stay with me? Or did she hope to sleep with him to further her literary career? Another possibility is she agreed to meet him, *not* sleep with him, and later publish an article on "how I spurned the most popular writer in small press history."

All I know for sure is too many people got the wrong impression of my role in the events that unraveled that weekend. It's my intention to set the record straight about what really happened between JW, Bukowski, and myself that weekend in San Francisco. It's important to know something about JW's background. JW and I both spent a considerable amount of time frequenting the former "Beatnik" haunts of North Beach. JW's experience was shorter than mine, since I was born in San Francisco and have lived here almost my entire life. During the time I was hanging out in North Beach I had little contact with JW. We drank at some of the same bars: The Coffee Gallery, Vesuvio's, Gino and Carlo's, Spec's, and the 1232 Club. But this was the extent of it.

JW may have been in the audience the night I was feature reader at the Coffee Gallery (paid $5 and all the beer I could drink). I remember two things about the reading: my holding out for imported German beer and a young woman telling me I "didn't look like a poet." I'm sure

Bukowski must have heard the same thing many times in his life.

From time to time I would run into JW at North Beach bars, but I never paid any particular attention to her. She was just one of hundreds of young women who hung around North Beach drinking, smoking grass, and experimenting with drugs.

The main difference between JW and the other women was that JW was intent on making a place for herself in the small press literary world, and was not above sleeping with North Beach poets and writers to achieve her goal. During her stay in San Francisco she had a brief affair with DP, a local poet and friend who edited a small literary magazine. During her stay in North Beach I can't ever recall speaking to her other than perhaps exchanging greetings. Later I would read a small book JW published titled *The North Beach Papers*, in which she described herself as a "nervous virgin." I don't know if this assessment is true or a self-serving statement. JW never seemed nervous to me. She was always in control of herself and knew exactly what she was doing.

The 70's were an exciting period in North Beach. There were regular poetry readings at the Intersection Art Center and numerous other bars and cafes. But it was across town (at the Ribeltod Vorden) where JW gave her first poetry reading. A reading she admits she "stumbled through."

The night she read at the Ribeltod Vorden, I was reading with Neeli Cherkovski at a cafe in North Beach. I read from the works of Wantling, while Cherkovski read from the works of d.a. levy, who years earlier had committed suicide. After our reading I went to the Ribeltod Vorden for a beer, but JW had already read her work and left. While her stay in North Beach lasted less than a year, she was a much talked about person. It was probably while staying with DP in North Beach that she became familiar with the work of Bukowski. DP's worship of Bukowski was second only to Steve Richmond and Neeli Cherkovski.

In *North Beach Papers,* JW said: "D. reading Bukowski to me/ cats and poems/ tumbled on the carpet/ into the bedroom/ doffing lights and clothes quickly/ hesitation is for liars." Even more revealing is the ending of the poem: "I travel into the City/ buy a carnation for my lapel/ sip my cappuccino/ last time I was here/ it took me a good two weeks/ to ruin D's love life/ this time/ less than forty-eight hours. Next time/ perhaps they'll learn to take Texas/ more seriously." Had I known JW's background and mindset when I met her in Texas at the Committee of Small Magazine Editors and Publisher's Conference (COSMEP), I might never have taken up with her.

From the first day of the conference, she seemed to focus her attention on me, perhaps because I edited and published *Second Coming*, or was on the board of directors of COSMEP, or maybe it was both. The board members were housed at the university dorms. It was hot and humid and difficult to sleep at night. Hi-fi music played through the paper-thin walls almost nonstop. There were no television sets. The only entertainment was watching cockroaches crawl across the dresser. When JW invited me to stay at her apartment, I didn't hesitate to accept her offer.

She wasn't the best-looking woman in town, but she was tall, lean, and had long legs. What followed was three days of heavy drinking, making love, and smoking grass. More drinking for me and more grass and hash for JW. The only drawback was having to put up with her friends who continually dropped by to see her, almost always unannounced. That they brought a wide assortment of alcoholic beverages with them didn't make up for their intrusion.

During the few times when JW wasn't stoned, I learned that in addition to working at the museum, she worked part-time for a wealthy Houston patron of the arts, who had inherited a family fortune. JW was more than willing to help him spend it. Her benefactor was a homosexual. Since JW always had a group of young boys hanging around her, it was a mutually beneficial situation for both of them. I learned JW's ambitions went far beyond being a part-time curator for a small Houston museum. The museum wanted to expand but lacked the funds to accomplish their goal. JW wanted me to persuade Bukowski to return to Houston and give another poetry reading. I told her she could use my name when she wrote Hank, but I wasn't going to ask him to give a reading. JW dropped the subject. We spent the days sweating in boring publishing workshops, the only pleasure coming from liquid lunches in air-conditioned bars.

The nights were different! Whatever else might be said about her, she was great in bed. The first night we made love, she told me every woman in America should be required to watch Linda Lovelace in *Deep Throat*. She didn't get an argument from me. My last night at the dorms before moving to her apartment, we made so much noise making love that we were the talk of the publishing conference. (I didn't realize two of the women COSMEP board members had a room directly below mine.)

After three days of high-intensity stimulants and constant sex, she drove me to the airport to catch my plane back to San Francisco. I agreed to write her when I returned home. She talked about visiting San Francisco, but I didn't want to commit myself. I've suffered from insomnia my entire adult life, but was so exhausted from the conference I somehow managed to fall asleep on the flight back home.

No matter how I might feel about JW, I do owe her a debt of gratitude for helping me see I was wasting my time serving on the COSMEP Board of Directors. COSMEP grew out of an early meeting between Jerry Burns and Len Fulton, two small press icons. In 1968, Fulton and Burns convinced eighty small press magazine editors and publishers to meet on the campus of U.C. Berkeley. For lack of a better name, Fulton and Burns called the meeting the "Conference of Small Magazine Editors and Publishers."

Fulton chaired a panel on distribution, something the small press magazines had never been able to achieve. Besides Fulton, the panel was made up of Harry Smith (*The Smith*), Douglas Blazek (*Ole Magazine*), D.R. Wagner (*Runcible Spoon)* and Hugh Fox (*Ghost Dance).* It was from this panel (which was seeking funds to print and distribute a catalog of small press publications) that COSMEP was born. A Board of Directors was appointed and membership soon grew to 110 dues-paying members. Richard Morris was hired as Director. He was ultimately given the responsibility of publishing the first "Catalog of Small Press Publications," which was typeset by Burns and printed by another small press veteran, Ben Hiatt, who was the publisher of *Grande Ronde Review.*

COSMEP soon became an activist organization that grew to over one thousand members. The membership was made up mostly of radical thinking small press people who fought to promote small press publications in opposition to the established academic monopoly of literature. But as the organization developed, dissent grew in its ranks. Ben Hiatt, one of the original founders, dropped out of COSMEP. In a letter to the membership, Hiatt said: "You gotta know that my feelings for a long while have been terribly hostile toward organizations in general, and publishing organizations in particular.

"We have become as slick as the New York publishing houses. Where in the hell are the crazy people that paved the way for all these slick magazines that dominate organizations like COSMEP? Obviously they can't operate in such a milieu even as I cannot. COSMEP is not the COSMEP that I knew and belonged to a few years ago."

Hiatt was right. As COSMEP grew, it began to be co-opted into the system through grants received from the Coordinating Council of Literary Magazines and the National Endowment For the Arts. The organization began to resemble the very same presses it had criticized as part of the establishment.

Ben Hiatt's resignation was followed by that of Kell Robertson, John Bennett, Carol Berge and others, who decided COSMEP no longer represented them. By then I was serving my third term as a board member and was rapidly becoming disillusioned. I watched the organization shift away from its original aims and goals by allowing non-literary magazines and presses into its ranks. The mimeo presses soon disappeared. With grant money in abundance, the small presses began publishing slick, commercial-looking magazines (including *Second Coming*). I had wrongfully assumed that if the product looked more professional, it would be easier to sell to the general public.

The simple truth is major bookstore chains refused to stock small press books and magazines. Small presses had to get their magazines and books distributed through small independent bookstores. The few stores that were sympathetic to the small press would only stock their books on consignment, and payment was more often than not slow or non-existent.

Paul Fericano and I secured a pilot NEA grant to purchase thirty small press book racks and put them in Northern California libraries. We had no problem getting libraries to accept the free book racks, and the response from the public was generally favorable. Our hope was that after the grant funding ended, the participating libraries would subscribe to the magazines and books the public had shown an interest in, but this never materialized.

The available government grant money was a curse in more ways that one. Many small presses who were turned down for grant money wrote angry letters and dropped out of publishing. A whole new in-group of small press publishers was being financed by the National

Endowment For the Arts, and its powerful Chairman of the Literature Program, Leonard Randolph. It wasn't long before COSMEP became a tool for Randolph's personal ambitions.

Once open only to literary small magazines and presses, COSMEP now openly solicited larger commercial publications. This changed an organization primarily concerned with better distribution for member presses to an organization largely dependent on federal grant assistance. When I was late to a board meeting in New York after stopping to listen to the concerns of several COSMEP members, I was loudly criticized in front of the membership. I responded by reminding the board I had been elected to serve the membership, not the board.

"COSMEP has lost its old-time spirit," John Pyros complained to me in private, just one of many members expressing their alienation from COSMEP. Ann Pride, a member of KNOW and publisher of a non-literary feminist press, spearheaded a feminist takeover of the COSMEP board. As more literary presses dropped out of COSMEP, they were replaced by non-literary presses. The discontent had actually begun years earlier when Lawrence Ferlinghetti resigned from the organization, citing the organization's courting of federal funds at a time when the Vietnam war was tearing America apart.

COSMEP was now feeding at the public trough in the most glutinous manner imaginable. Worse yet, COSMEP had very few minority presses in its ranks and was doing nothing to make them welcome. Hugh Fox wrote an angry letter to the board: "We've become another corporate org. I've realized what an absolute bullshit organization it's become, and how vital, important, significant it *could* be."

Founder Len Fulton exited the organization in 1975 only to return twenty years later and, as Chairman, ended the corporation's days. "I saw it born and I saw it die," said Fulton. "Born was better."

I grew tired of battling with a board of directors who conducted its affairs as if the members had given them a mandate to rule instead of serve. When Judy Hogan was elected by the board as Chairperson, she frequently called Randolph on the telephone asking for his input on how much grant money to seek and how to write the grant proposal.

The COSMEP board successfully lobbied to have Mary MacArthur, a board member, appointed to the NEA Literature Panel. Hugh Fox and I were the only board members to protest the action as being a conflict of interest. COSMEP began to rely more heavily on the NEA for support, even though the organization had over 1,000 dues-paying members contributing $20 a year. Despite this COSMEP was unable to pay a $35 booth fee at the 1976 San Francisco Book Fair. The spirit of the 60's was dead, replaced by splits between factions. Board members had become politicians openly taking partisan positions. The unity and brotherhood that had existed in 1968 had turned into dissenting factions opposed to and intolerant of each other.

The defining event leading to my resignation was the board's refusal to publish (in the *COSMEP Newsletter*) a member's letter criticizing the board. I strongly protested the board's action. Hugh Fox again wrote: "My friends, you successfully blocked Todd Lawson's letter from getting printed in the *COSMEP Newsletter* because it offended you. I didn't write him and join with him in initiating action against COSMEP (with the help of the ACLU) because it had violated his constitutional rights (First Amendment of the Bill of Rights) of Freedom of Speech. Perhaps I should have. But let me swear this, that if COSMEP moves any closer than it already is toward becoming an *instrument of repression and censorship*, I'll destroy it, even if it means getting in a car and driving around the U.S. and talking to the 1,000 members personally." When Fox, a liberal Professor at Michigan State University, left the U.S. on a one-year sabbatical, the board tried to unseat him. They failed by a single vote.

When the board attacked me for not supporting its position on accepting an NEA grant for a van distribution project, Richard Morris (the Director) incurred their wrath when he supported me in a letter to the board: "I feel disappointed about the NEA's decision on the van project too. In effect, Judy [the chair] worked out a deal with the NEA, according to which we would keep our request down to a totally inadequate $60,000 in return for a chance to get two vans. If the NEA only wanted to fund one van, they should have given us a chance to have it where we thought it would have the best chance and that would be the West Coast." The original request called for one NEA-financed van and the hiring of a van driver to travel to selected West Coast cities, with the intention of exhibiting small press books and magazines. Promotion was the primary aim of the project, with distribution a secondary goal.

Mary MacArthur, a board member on the NEA Literature Panel who had strong East Coast ties, successfully pushed to modify the grant request to include two vans: one for the West Coast and one for the East Coast. However, no additional funds were provided for the second van, thereby dooming the project to certain failure. Fox, Morris and myself argued that Randolph and the NEA wanted the project to fail. We represented a small but growing minority who distrusted the motives of the NEA.

The die was cast. The board was now allowing Randolph to sit in on board meetings and make decisions that were not in the best interests of the organization. Back home on my own turf, I searched my soul and wrote a poem for JW titled "COSMEP Conference Poem."

> **Everyone back home in San Francisco asks me**
> **Why don't you write poetry anymore?**
> **I keep telling them it's because**
> **I prefer friends**
> **My enemies can't accept this**
> **But they're boring for the most part**
> **Most of them are editors and publishers**
> **Or running for re-election**
> **To the COSMEP board of directors.**
> **What's become of you they insist**
> **You dress so "spiffy"**
> **And what's a city dude like you**
> **Doing listening to C and W music?**
> **And didn't Bukowski write and say**
> **That Wantling was slipping fast**
> **And that his work was never that good**
> **To begin with?**
> **And didn't Wantling write me and say**
> **Be selfish with your talent**
> **The rest is a fucking waste of time?**
> **I mean all this organizational shit**
> **Is starting to get to me**
>
> **Hugh Fox has flipped out in Spain**
> **And Judy says that I'm a passionate man**
> **And Anne Pride and I have grown**

Too tired to fight anymore
And Mary MacArthur gives us
A 4-star rating for our bed performance
Heard down below in the Women's Dorm
I guess that's all people listen to anymore
And Ruth Gottstein is a book fair addict
And Jackie Eubanks is running for
The Library Hall of Fame while
Richard Morris plays Don Juan
In a new play smuggled into
The Texas University Dorms

Oh if they only knew about
The other side of life
The lows and highs
The laughter the caressing
Of a sofa's leg
2 joints into and 20 minutes
From the airport

COSMEP 1968 provided new blood
To a dying vein
Now it's book fairs and
A $30,000 National Endowment
For the arts bookmobile
And mafia cut out comic books
From an organization called
The Coordinating Council
Of Literary Magazines

I stand alone on cold nights
Hearing the voices
Of a thousand suicides
My hands heavy as a hammer
Refuse to build
A new bridge of words
Caught in Austin Texas
With a constant hard on

In between the talking
About organizational politics
And all the other shit that doesn't
Belong between the sheets
But that's what organizations
Do to you.

All around me my friends dying
And not even knowing it
Their dreams melting like wax
The survivors playing the game
By the rules
All poets should learn
To complain without suffering

There ain't no Shaman poets left
They died with the Platters
And the Great Pretender
Paper tigers tripping over
Fragile egos
Oh they come out of the closet
To hear themselves read
They read the longest
And say the least
And never stay long enough
To hear other poets read

And selling out isn't so much a sin
As the small price they place
On themselves
But still sometimes
It seems worth it
Finding someone stamped in
The same mold
Harry Smith is still in
There fighting though
Plimpton says he's done more
Than anyone else

To ruin literature
And tops it off by saying:
Come on Harry we're all Gentlemen
And Len Fulton ain't given up the ship
And A. D. isn't likely to
It's just that the pirates now
Outnumber the crew

My veins keep exploding with
Each new disappointment
My tongue senses
The hopelessness
Far better it trace the path
Down a woman's belly
Than seek an image without
A climax

I have seen your face
In the darkness
Of death's shadow
Free from the pressure
And demands of those
Who would use and
Attack you
To hide their own inadequacies

I have felt the softness
Of your fingers caress
My chest
Your tongue a soft feather
On my spine
Wrapped together like
Christmas paper
While a half-mile down
The campus
An editor and former friend
Says nice to see you
Have a good trip home

When what he really means
Is hope the plane runs
Into rough weather
But to ease his guilt
Wishes me only a broken spirit

A short time before
The airplane leaves
You remind me that
I'm the oldest man
You've ever slept with
And neither of us knows why
Only that it's better than
Roberts Rules of Order
Or by-laws that get some
People off

They play taps
At Arlington Cemetery
In the name
Of national pride
But it takes
Flesh and bone
To breathe electricity into
A man's balls
The rest is played
With mirrors and illusion

Ten years from now
I will have no visions
Of organizations
Or those who ran them
So I write you this poem
Remembering an intensity
Too long forgotten
The moving in and out
The making of a perfect poem
If only for the briefest
Moment

Let the politicians
Full of pesticides for thoughts
Dwell beneath dying trees
Each word they echo
A chain saw cutting away
At the seeds of life
The true poet's body filled
With the spirit of life
A child waiting
To be reborn

I dedicate this poem
To you
Our bodies like
Beached ships
Shaking beneath clear blue
Coral reefs.

Hank read the poem in Harry Smith's *Newsletter* and was quick to praise it. He told me he didn't like political poems, but that my poem had gotten through to him. He urged me to get out of the politics of poetry and devote my energy to writing. Not long afterwards, I resigned from the COSMEP board of directors. In a letter Richard Morris published in the *COSMEP Newsletter*, I spoke out against the unholy alliance COSMEP had entered into with the NEA. Michael Mooney, a respected East Coast author, commented on my resignation from COSMEP.

"The worst of this, and what is most shameful, is how well the deceits worked on those who first of all wanted the best for literature," Mooney said. "Your explanation of why you resigned from COSMEP is both fine itself, and sad. It says clearly the decent things. It speaks up for writing too."

After my return from Texas, JW wrote to tell me Hank had visited her in Houston. She was disappointed she had not been able to be alone with him. She said Hank had cut his leg in an accident and was on antibiotics which had prevented him from drinking. She had given him some "downers" to ease his pain. She said she and several friends had gone on a bar-hopping spree that lasted into the early morning hours.

JW said Hank "scored" with one of the young groupies and that she had allowed Hank and the young woman to stay overnight at her apartment. I tried to imagine JW listening to the squeaking bedsprings in the guest room, wondering if Hank was as good as his reputation.

JW telephoned me to say she was flying to San Francisco to attend a party I was throwing to celebrate the publication of the *Second Coming California Bicentennial Poets Anthology*. I told her it would be nice to have her at the party and while I couldn't help with her expenses, she was welcome to stay with me. JW laughed and said her airplane ticket had already been taken care of. I didn't ask for details. Shortly afterwards she flew to San Francisco and I picked her up at the airport. We had a couple of drinks at the airport bar. I began to feel uncomfortable about the situation. JW was all over me and talking as if we were "going steady." We were good in bed together but I had never given her reason to believe our relationship would go beyond the physical. After we finished our drinks, I drove her to her brother's place, which wasn't far from where I lived. He wasn't home but her friend N was. The three of us chatted in the kitchen for an hour or more, getting high on tequila and beer chasers.

N wasn't my type of woman and I had heard rumors that JW's brother was on drugs. It seemed like everyone in San Francisco was experimenting with drugs. As long as they weren't dealing, I had no objections. Feeling a buzz on, I excused myself and headed home for a few hours of rest. JW accompanied me but we didn't make love that night. I had made plans to drive north to Mendocino early in the morning, and JW seemed excited about the trip. We got up early the next morning and had a cup of coffee before making the trip.

When we reached the coast I rented a small place near the beach before driving to nearby Fort Bragg for a few rounds of drinks. That night we had a quiet seafood dinner at Nojo Village, and consumed several more drinks before returning to our room for a night of intense lovemaking. It was as good or better than it had been in Texas. In the morning we had breakfast at a nearby lodge before driving along Highway One to explore an old fort that had been remodeled for the tourist trade. We made love outside the fort, in the bright sunlight, neither of us caring that someone might come by and catch us in the act. We left early that day for San Francisco. There were still twenty-four hours left before the party, but there was a lot of work to do.

JW was caught up in the beauty of my Laidley Street apartment, which overlooked downtown San Francisco with a sweeping view of the entire Bay Area. It wasn't really an apartment but an extension of the landlord's home, which was separate from the main house. The apartment had an outside balcony with access to the landlord's back yard. JW couldn't believe I was only paying $300 a month rent, which at times I found hard to believe myself.

I didn't get much sleep that night between making love and listening to the crazy rooster crow next door. Whoever said that roosters crow only in the morning sure as hell didn't know what they were talking about. The rooster was more than its usual obnoxious self that night. Unable to sleep, I put on a pair of jeans and walked to the back yard, where I discovered my alcoholic next-door neighbor calling the rooster: "Here Allan . . . Here Allan . . . Here Allan." The nut had named the rooster after me.

The telephone never stopped ringing all evening. Some of the calls were from well-wishers, others from people I preferred to keep away from. JW was amused at the number of people who kept calling. Finally I had to turn off the telephone, not wanting to talk to another poet, not then, maybe not ever.

Tomasita, the landlord's black cat, paid us a visit. I opened the sliding patio door window and let her inside. When JW reached down to pet her, the cat recoiled and scratched her arm, leaving a nasty mark for her to take home to Houston. Perhaps I should have seen it as an omen of things to come.

The next morning I drove JW to N's place and returned to my apartment to prepare for the party. JW hitched a ride to the party, which was being held at the home of Bil Paul, a friend of mine who frequently contributed photographs to the magazine. The party was filled with poets, would-be poets, painters and photographers, many of whom were contributors to the anthology. Jack Micheline got drunk and screamed and hollered a lot. He was by far the most interesting person at the party. Ben Hiatt drove down from Sacramento and tried to put the make on JW. Harold Norse came clutching a copy of *Hustler* magazine in his arms. He seemed wired and nervous. The magazine had just published a short story of his and he was upset because the editor had used a black and white contributor's photo instead of color.

Bob Kaufman was reciting poetry off the top of his head. Kaye McDonough, the Zelda of North Beach who would later bear the son of Gregory Corso, looked as majestic as always. Kell Robertson showed up dressed in his usual cowboy hat and jeans, sporting dark sunglasses, trying his damnedest to live up to the image of his magazine *Desperado*.

In many ways it was the party to end all parties, even by San Francisco standards. The kitchen was stacked with every conceivable brand of booze. There was Texas-style chili, ham, cheese, fresh vegetables, veggie dips, fruit and potato salad, topped off by a twenty-five pound cake with "California Poets" written in baby-blue icing. It would cost me a good sum of money, but I wanted it to be a party people would remember.

After the party was over, JW and I bid farewell to the remaining stragglers, many of whom Bil Paul was kind enough to put up for the night. We returned to my apartment weighed down with so much food and booze that both sex and sleep were impossible.

The next morning JW startled me when she told me Hank had paid her fare to San Francisco. She seemed to think it was funny. The great one paying her way to San Francisco while she stayed with me. Hank of course would never have agreed to pay had he known her intentions. She and N were to pick him up at the airport, stop off at a bar or two for drinks, and then drive to N's where Hank would stay the night. I was annoyed she had waited so long to tell me about Hank paying for her trip to San Francisco. We had a heated argument. The first and only fight we had. JW felt I was jealous about Hank staying at N's house and swore she did not plan to sleep with him. I don't know if I was jealous or not. I probably was.

After breakfast I drove JW to N's pad, hardly speaking to her for the entire trip. When I pulled the car over to let her out, she kissed me on the side of the cheek and asked if I was still going to pick her up in the morning. She wanted to spend her last day in San Francisco with me. I have to admit she had a way of turning a man's thoughts inside out.

The next day I was surprised to receive a telephone call from Hank. He was at the airport sharing a drink with JW and N while waiting for his flight back to Los Angeles. He apologized for coming to San

Francisco and seeing JW behind my back. He said it wasn't his intention to move in on me and didn't know she was staying with me at my apartment. I told him I had been in the dark myself up until the last minute. I didn't know whom to be more pissed off at. Should I have been angry at JW for her deception? At Hank, who surely must have come to San Francisco to put the make on JW? You don't pay a woman's airfare to another city to sit around and chat.

Hank broke down and told me that the whole twenty-four hours with JW had been a living hell. He said that after an evening of heavy drinking, arguing, and name-calling, he had been forced to go up a ladder and sleep alone in a tiny loft space. Hank said JW was too grim for him, but that the whole thing had been more his fault than hers. We exchanged a few more words before he had to hang up and catch his plane back to Los Angeles. On his return home Hank wrote and said he probably had a wrong read on things. He had been too drunk that night in San Francisco and tended to get scared at times like this, seeing only potential trouble ahead. He ended by saying he had various ghosts chewing at him that night and it had been one of the worst evenings he ever experienced with a woman.

In my heart I suspected both Hank and JW were equally to blame for what took place. There weren't any innocent parties. I recalled how John Bryan's wife (Joanie) and Wantling's wife (Ruthie) lent evidence that Hank wasn't above trying to score with a friend's woman. I thought back to an earlier letter from Hank in which he discussed his first meeting with JW.

Hank said: "Caught good rays from her right off. I longed to be alone with her, but I was with somebody else and she had a boyfriend at the time, but I'm glad you had some luck with her. She's a lady and a feeling person. You should try to follow up your good luck. Women like her simply don't abound everywhere. I was never as impressed on a first meeting with a woman than I was with JW. You know what I mean." I knew full well what he meant, having felt much the same way about JW when I first met her in Austin. Those feelings changed after her weekend with me in San Francisco. But there you had it, in Hank's own words, saying how much he admired JW and how lucky I was to have found her. If this was the case, why did he pay her airplane fare to meet him in San Francisco?

I've never been able to get an accurate read on the events leading up to that weekend in San Francisco. Hank saw fit to bring her name up several times in correspondence. Not long after flying home, Hank wrote and said: "I just ain't got it anymore, Kid. No, I really didn't go up to cut you out. JW still has plenty, you know that better than I. JW still has a fine flow to her. I do think, though, that she's a little too grim for me. Maybe she's not around you. I hope not."

Two weeks later, another letter arrived in the mail: "Sorry on JW, I probably took a wrong reading. I was too drunk anyhow. And I get scared. I think, God, yet more trouble. She's a very fine girl."

A month later, still another letter arrived: "Take a plane and go lie down next to JW for a week. Eat breakfast together and get drunk at night."

After reading JW's published article confessing to the events of that weekend, Hank wrote and said: "JW has every right to write about me. I really flunked that night. Sometimes it's the conditions. I believe if it had been at my place it might have worked differently. Or maybe not. I have no excuses."

I had long since put the incident out of my mind when, four years later, Hank wrote and said: "I didn't want to say anything about JW to you while you were going with her, but when I met her up North I sensed a heavy deadness there. It stuck out all over her. The decision not to have sex with her was not entirely hers. I passed, feeling relief. Just to let you know." Why this change of sentiment? Why continue to bring up the subject? Future letters had occasional unkind references to JW. They say love and hate are kin. How much love and how much hate was there? What was the real truth? I knew the answer lay somewhere between what Hank said and what JW wrote in "Poetess Tells All: The Day Bukowski Fell In Love With Me."

I spent the last twenty-four hours of JW's visit listening to her version of how she rejected Hank that night at N's pad. JW said Hank had gotten drunk and they spent most of the evening in the kitchen in what she called "a battle of wills," testing each other's strength. According to JW, the vibes had grown heavy with N and JW's brother trying to convince her that it would be good for her literary career to sleep with Hank. She and Hank remained in the kitchen drinking and arguing until nearly three in the morning when Hank broke down and started crying, telling JW that he was in love with her.

She admitted being hostile and belligerent and shouting at Hank,

"You don't even know me! You can't be in love with me." I tried to picture Hank climbing up that ladder leading to the loft and going to sleep alone. On JW's last night in San Francisco we made love several times in the loft where Hank had slept twenty-four hours earlier. When I woke up the next morning I wondered about JW's motives for making love to me in the loft she had forced Hank to sleep alone in.

As time passed I came to the conclusion JW felt she could gain more recognition as the woman who "didn't" go to bed with Bukowski than just another mark on his scorecard. JW never made it big, either in the commercial mainstream or in the small presses, but few people do.

Thirteen

With the JW affair behind me I wrote and asked Hank if he wanted to be part of a special *Second Coming* issue featuring the work of Bukowski, myself, and a former San Quentin Prison poet Ed "Foots" Lipman. Lipman had gained the nickname "Foots" from his size 14 feet and was known for his escapes from Texas prisons. He was a 34-year-old who served time in Texas and California prisons for armed robbery. During a daring escape from a Texas jail, Lipman had left the sheriff tied to the commode, hardly endearing himself to the law enforcement community. Many of his friends compared him to the movie character portrayed by Paul Newman in "Cool Hand Luke."

Lipman was not your usual prison inmate. He was a member of Mensa. He served time at Folsom and at San Quentin where an infected leg and a botched prison hospital operation left him nearly crippled. Lipman wrote in an early letter how difficult it had been for him to learn to walk again, and how he kept falling, never sure about stairs or who might be sneaking up on him. While recovering from his operation in the prison hospital, he sent me a poem:

My hospital bed watches
the nurses come and go:
they fuss over tubes and bandages.
I worry about their concern;
they talk loudly
but it doesn't help.
and then one morning
a beautiful one
brings the medicine
in a soft hand and her smile
is real.
(her breath faintly touched
with orange peel and the rest

of her smells of sunshine
and green places)
Suddenly I want to get up
to wobble the hall
steadied at first
by those soft hands
and pushed each slow step
by pain
and that smile.

When I told him he didn't seem to fit the stereotyped image of a hardened criminal, Lipman said it hadn't always been that way. There was a time when he was young, reckless and considered dangerous. He ended his letter with a poem:

Eulogy For Chinaman

I really
didn't believe he'd burn me
wasn't worth it hardly
y'know
but that ounce got too heavy
for him
took me 3 almost whole weeks
to find his pad
I don't think he'll burn at least me again
although I hated to see his chick cry
it almost changed my mind

After reading his poem, "Nights Primarily 111," I decided to publish a small chapbook of poems titled *No Capital Crime.*

Nights Primarily 111

the TV echoes
into my cell
I can almost make
the words
at count time
a man shines
a flashlight
thru steel bars
to reassure the
people (& the warden)
that they got
this poet:

they got this poet
only by flashlight
they got this poet.

No longer considered an escape risk, Lipman was paroled to painfully limp the streets of San Francisco with the assistance of a cane. Less than a year after his release from prison, he was found dead under suspicious circumstances in his small San Rafael apartment. The authorities found a poem left on the nightstand next to his bed:

I know that Dennis
is cold now
(he was always cold
on the hottest days)
But now he's gone
so far away
none of us can hold his arm
or hear his singing.
(the days he had
are now willed to others;
I must refuse, to live)

Dennis dead, impossible
to realize
but always expected -
he'd left no doubt
about coming back inside:
"better to move fast/& burn out
than move slowly/& smoulder"
And now the Earth
has him as cold
as sooner or later
she'll have us all.

Lipman was found tucked in bed with two hundred dollar bills lying on top of the bedroom dresser. Rumor was that he died from an OD and the money was left there by friends to help cover the funeral expenses. Another rumor was that he had pulled one last caper, acting as the driver for a holdup and had died in bed after his heart gave out on him. There was no evidence found to support the theory of a drug OD, and the second rumor is the stuff legends are made of. But it's quite possible that his heart did give out on him. Yet how does one explain the $200 left on the bedroom dresser?

Whatever the situation I decided to honor Lipman with a special edition of *Second Coming*. Because he had no substantial literary reputation, I decided the best way to showcase his work would be to include it alongside the work of Bukowski. I would round out the issue with my own work. Hank agreed to participate in the special issue. Not long afterwards poems and letters flowed between us and our friendship grew stronger.

In his letters Hank seldom failed to mention problems with women, and many of his recollections were material for later short stories. The accounts were never dull. Like the time he met a redhead and two young women who were passing through Los Angeles. Hank said he wound up sleeping with all three and that, unlike his experience with JW, the affair left him with happy memories. "It was good in many ways. I guess I'm just an old letch," he said.

Hank's story reminded me of my own wild times. My first experience with a threesome occurred while I was attending City College of

San Francisco and working part-time at the Rincon Annex post office. Jack Fineager and I lived in the same apartment building on Pierce Street on the fringe of a high crime area. Jack was fifteen years older than me but had the energy of a much younger man.

One morning he knocked on my door unshaven and disheveled. He said a female nymphomaniac friend of his was visiting from Los Angeles and she was wearing him out. He begged me to take her out for the evening so he could get some sleep. When I protested I didn't have the money, he said this wasn't a problem. The woman had recently won a large divorce settlement from her well-off husband, and would foot the bill.

Always horny, I agreed to date her. She was no stranger to San Francisco and knew a stripper who worked at a downtown club, where we spent the last part of the night drinking watered-down drinks. After the club closed we went back to my apartment for drinks, but for some reason I couldn't talk her into bed. She kept insisting we go downstairs and wake Jack up. I finally gave in to her demands and knocked loudly on Jack's door. I was surprised when he opened the door fully dressed and welcomed us in.

Now that I look back on it, I shouldn't have been surprised. I think they planned it that way. After a round of drinks we wound up in bed together. It was pure craziness! There were hands everywhere and you didn't know whom the hands belonged to. I soon found myself getting a head job, and could only hope it was from the woman. When I woke up the next morning Jack's friend was under the covers, giving me a blow job. I looked across the room and saw Jack sitting on the sofa reading the Sunday morning comic strips. For all the publicity it got, I don't think Hank's love life was any more bizarre than mine.

In a follow-up letter Hank said, "I think that when I lose it is when I begin to believe, not a total belief, but a bit of belief, like a dwarfed and crippled Christianity. I'm nailed to this fucking lamp shade with these paper clips."

In a telephone conversation we discussed how gratifying it was to watch a young woman in a halter and summer shorts strolling down the street with painted nails, swinging hips, and pouting lips. We both agreed that the swing of the right woman's hips offered more promise than an audition with God. Hank said it would be heaven if such women never put on weight, never lost their sensual smile, never grew weary from time or betrayals, never settled for a husband and baby, a box of chocolates, and long afternoons looking at soap operas.

Hank's ideal woman was someone who would never give up her wiggle. He later sent me a poem expressing these exact sentiments, and I had to wonder if he had not been quoting from it when we talked on the telephone.

At the time the special Lipman issue was being put together, Hank was seeing a woman he referred to as "Cupcakes." She was a tall redhead whom Hank claimed would be the death of him. He promised to send me a poem he had written about her and said once I read it, I would know what he meant.

In September 1976, Hank sent me several poems for consideration in the special Lipman issue, including his "Cupcakes" poem, and brought up the subject of our meeting at one of his readings in San Francisco.

"It was good to see you at that reading," Hank said. "There is something about your face that is much more different than the average poetic San Francisco face."

Hank was feeling depressed, and said the redhead he had been in love with, a part-time hooker, told him she was going back to practice her trade. Hank said she had turned a trick the night before and he had cashed a check for her for a hundred dollars and hoped it wouldn't bounce. He said while he was luckier than most men when it came to women, he doubted there was a real woman out there for him.

"I'll probably go to my deathbed without ever seeing her, which hardly makes my life different from other men. Yet I keep feeling that maybe she's out there somewhere, but how do I find her?" Hank ended his letter by saying, "Jesus Christ, make it on out here, Kid, and keep the contact. The years shorten upon the same mirror." In a later telephone conversation he talked about his continued troubles with "Cupcakes." Hank said the main problem was she was a "pill head" and past experience had shown him that people on speed become hard and jaded over time. She would eventually break up with Hank, leaving a void that would take months to fill. In the meantime, the poems and correspondence continued. I had put my own life pretty much in order, which caused Hank to write and say:

"As per your letters, you seem to have your lifestyle and thoughts pretty much in order. You're wiser than I am. I expect too much. Too many miracles. As long as I have lived, I ought to realize that the plot isn't going to change. Ma Barker knew what to do."

As time passed Hank began to grow weary of the Lipman project and uneasy about my rejecting a good number of his poems. They simply were not his best work. The submission process continued, and Hank pleaded with me to tell him when he could stop sending poems.

I had already selected the cover as well as my own work and Lipman's poems. I only needed a few more poems from Bukowski to complete the issue. Hank said: "Since the other poet (Ed Lipman) is dead and most likely to remain that way, it might be an O.K. gesture to let him have most of the pages. His last poetic hard-on, after all. What do you think?" A short time later he called and said he was experiencing trouble with women again. I could tell from the sound of his voice that he had been drinking. Suddenly he let out a loud curse and I could hear a crash of considerable magnitude. It turned out that the legs on Hank's typewriter stand had given way and his trusted typewriter had fallen on the floor. Hank said he would call back later, but he never did.

A few days later I received a letter from him riddled with typing errors. He explained he was having difficulty with the "O" key, which apparently was damaged when the typewriter hit the floor. Hank said he was trying to get over his failed love affair and that he had written a poem for me, which was in the mail. The poem arrived a few days later. I took my car to the gas station for an oil change and left the poem on the front seat. I walked two blocks to a nearby bar. When I returned the poem was gone. No one at the gas station admitted seeing it.

I wrote Hank and told him someone had stolen the poem he sent and asked him to please send another copy. Shortly afterwards he sent a copy of the poem and said, "Here's the stolen poem. Do you think it was Neeli?" I think it is more likely it was the guy who pumped gas. These were the kind of people Hank wrote poems for. I imagined the poem hanging in a dimly lit room in some rundown hotel. Maybe the only possession the guy valued. Hank wrote again and asked how close I was to finishing the selection of poems. He again talked about his disappointment in love.

"I am still mending from the Cupcakes disaster. It's a slow heal. The eternal beautiful witch factor. She is killing some other poor sucker's soul even as I write this," Hank said. "Some people need to kill. It's an instinct. It keeps their juices flowing."

Hank asked if I thought I would ever be able to step away from editing and publishing. "Can you get the editor bug out of your system?" he asked. He said I should seriously give it a try "before the dogs eat off your toes. There aren't any poets, gather real valuables. Get the hell out of North Beach and go East of no West. Allah be with you."

In November 1976 I received a letter complaining about sending so many poems for the special Lipman issue. Hank wanted to put poetry aside and begin working on his third novel as soon as a visiting Canadian bellydancer departed. That night I sat down and made my final selection from the poems he sent, and wrote to tell him he could begin work on his novel.

A day later I discovered a long letter from Lipman after his transfer from San Quentin to Folsom Prison. He spoke about small press publishing, prison life, and some of the same people we knew. He talked in detail about his impending release.

"I have my priorities in better shape this time around. This joint does at least that; you damn sure best figure out what's real and what is not because it doesn't take but one more fall and you might as well lie down to rest for awhile, this time more likely for good. But, no matter, cause that's what I'd call an extremely remote possibility, since we both know full well where it's really at, all the myths and lies and distortions aside.

"I'm going to the Parole Board in March, looks favorable this time. I mean, it's only been 10 fucking years and 2 fucking months, right? And I didn't kill anyone to begin with, in fact I never hurt anyone. Except myself. But they tend to forget that particular fact each year.

"However, all being said and done, my being to some degree crippled this time has a positive effect on my chances; they figure my crime days are over since I can't move fast enough, or run at all; except for what they call my 'mastermind possibilities,' which I think is absurd. I tell them to look at my jacket, what the fuck did I ever mastermind, having been stumbling around like a blind man most of my adult life, and all of the rest."

Here was a man who had spent fifteen of his brief thirty-four years on earth behind prison walls. He was a legend among the prison population, many of whom compared him to McMurphy, the unyielding protagonist of *One Flew Over the Cuckoo's Nest.*

As these thoughts swirled around inside my head, I composed a memorial poem I used to close the special Bukowski/Lipman/Winans issue.

For Foots

here behind the walls
of san quentin
the seeds were planted
took root and grew into
rock
behind these walls
the words gave birth
smothered with visions
of gargoyle guards
and damned spirits
walking the exercise yard
like earth worms wiggling
on a hook.

I heard of your death
at 12:30 a.m
Monday night, September
the eighth
it made me so angry
and sick that I walked
the balcony
a little mad
a little drunk
tears frozen
the saliva choked up
empty inside
the stars a silent prayer
clothed in darkness
each heart beat one closer
to yours

all those god damn years
behind those walls
free but 3 months
the body come home
to a black box
Big Ed
I'm storing up images
of you
they file so easily into
the slots of my soul
the pain an anchor
in the sea of death.
Your poems delicate astute
full of life

I remember the one about
you pulling clods of grass
from the earth and tossing
them at a passing train
the one called
BECAUSE SAN QUENTIN
KILLED TWO MORE TODAY
and still the killings go on
even after the release
after the deadly boredom
that stifles and maims
the imagination

The butcher prison doctors
who left you crippled
for life
the outside needle of death
bringing the ultimate fix
the seeds of destruction
planted by the guardians
of the State
and Jack Micheline's voice
on the telephone

shaken with tears
forced to witness another
death each one bringing
us closer to our own

This poem is for you
Ed
not the academics who
will find fault with
its internal structure
like you at times rough
unpolished but honest
each word dying its own
slow death

In the Buddhist temple
of life
all living things must die
there is no survival
no I Ching philosophy
tarot cards horoscopes
or magic incantations
to bring back the dead

Big Ed
I'm taking a ride with
You through my head
The harsh wind carrying
The ashes of your spirit
Across the field of life

You're very much alive
in my thoughts tonight
I can't seem to shake
you loose

All night the bruises
lay heavy beneath

the skin where
the pain dies hardest

murderers shrink back
into the shadows
law men quiver in fear
too soon too many forget
how easy it is to allow
the vision to slip from
the mind, loose thread
threading a fine needle
the amnesia diminishing
the scale of truth
but your words linger on
your deeds recorded into
the minds of men this
state will never understand

The earth peels back
its cracked lips
and howls for her children
to be heard
There is a strange code
to this language we are
addicted to
Evil spelled backwards is
LIVE
Dying is in its whole
the disintegration
the bacterial feeding
a live process
and so your spirit lives on
even as I retreat back
to the depths of my being
listening as you did
to the blood beat solid
against the eyes and hands
knowing there are secrets

in the blood that cannot
be denied or sold out to
the whims and dreams
of others.

Sleep well brother
Only the flesh is gone
Your private strength
Lives on in all of us

I later asked Hank if he would consider giving a poetry reading in San Francisco with Jack Micheline, Alta and myself. Hank wrote back and said:

"My spiritual advisors have told me not to give any more mixed readings. But shit, they are a bring-down. I like Alta, you and Jack, but it just wouldn't work. It causes a scratching that I don't like, so I have to say no. Call me a shit, but there's a lot of shit in the river."

I understood his position, having once written Joan Baez to ask her to write a blurb for the back cover of my book *The Reagan Psalms*. Her mother responded on her behalf and said her daughter had made a decision long ago not to write forewords for books because "it would open the floodgates." The same held true for Hank. In his letter, Hank again praised Micheline:

"Micheline has never received his just due, but it's just as well. It'll keep him on his springs instead of turning him into a silky-haired, over-read, precious Norman Mailer. Overexposure is the toughest whore of them all, and one few men can turn away from."

Hank ended his letter by saying how badly he missed the belly-dancer. "We laughed for almost nine days and nights. She said that I caused the laughter, but it was her. She made me feel good and crazy. Sometimes there's luck. When there is, you stock up on it and wait for the other times."

Following the publication of the special Lipman issue, Hank requested I send a copy to a certain German publisher.

"I think the Germans have me down as a mixture of Bogart, Hemingway, Adolph [Hitler] and Jack the Ripper," Hank said. "I may go there this summer with my lady friend. Drink and die there. The

Fatherland." I mailed three copies of the special issue to the German publisher and sent Hank several additional copies.

Except for a brief conversation in which Hank said his life consisted mainly of "booze, women, writing and the race track," there followed a period in which we lost contact. I was burned out from editing and publishing and working full-time for the San Francisco Art Commission's Neighborhood Arts Program, where I was employed as an editor and writer under the federally-funded Comprehensive Employment Training Act (CETA).

The politics of the job were unbelievable. I was one of two hundred out of two thousand applicants selected for one of the coveted CETA art positions. Politics aside, I was grateful for the freedom the job gave me to write and publish and not worry about where my next dollar came from. The job also gave me the time to continue *Second Coming*'s commitment to prison poets as well as teaching poetry at separate San Mateo County Junior High Schools.

The crowning achievement of the arts job was the 1980 Poets and Music Festival, a presentation of poetry and music honoring the late poet Josephine Miles, the blues great John Lee Hooker, and poet and political activist Roberto Vargas. During this time I broke the silence between Hank and me. I told him I was feeling depressed, which resulted in a quick response.

"You sound down. It's probably those big mouths down there proclaiming their greatness. The longer I know these poets the more sick I believe they are. Asking for decency and love and understanding from the world in their poems, and in person being exactly the opposite of what they ask for."

By this time Hank had pretty much settled in with Linda Lee and said, "Getting fucked by many is not so important; it's a settling for an easy clarity that I think helps the nights, the days, the months."

Hank and I agreed about how petty San Francisco poets can be, and I believe this only helped our friendship. Hank said I was one of the few San Francisco poets he felt comfortable with. The truth is I never fit into the San Francisco poetry mold and have no desire to.

In his letter, Hank said things were relatively quiet. He seemed content to settle down with Linda Lee, whom he met at the Troubadour night club in Hollywood. We discussed *Second Coming*'s place in literary history. The reviews had always been good and I had never experienced any trouble obtaining submissions from talented poets and writers. However, at times I questioned the importance of keeping the magazine going.

"*Second Coming* is *always* good," Hank said, "and that includes the Winans, jailbird dead, Buk issue. Yours is one of only two or three good magazines in existence. It's that simple and you know it. And you, as a person, have nothing of the old poet bullshit about you. I think you know that too."

I credit Hank for giving me the assurance I needed to keep on writing and publishing during difficult periods in my life. Without our friendship, I might have found it easier to throw in the towel, like so many other poets I have known. Poets who gave up the written word for a life of alcohol and drugs, or a comfortable life in the suburbs.

"It isn't always easy," as Philip Levine said in a letter to me. "It's nice to know you're still in poetry. So many people my age or yours get discouraged and wind up in one hell or another."

In his letter Hank said he was drinking three or four bottles of wine a night, playing the piano, and had just completed his novel (*Women*), which had 99 chapters and was 433 typed pages long. He was convinced *Women* was his best book, but said John Martin was going to hold off publishing it because a new book of Hank's poems (*Love is a Dog from Hell*) had just been released. Hank felt he was "near the edge," producing twenty to thirty poems a week.

"I hope the food and the skies and the girls are being good to you, but always remember that betrayal is a built-in concept of the way it goes. The blade will never be as sharp when you know that it's been there."

He had been on a drinking spree, and offered me some advice: "Get on the white wine, A.D. Beer is fattening and the hard stuff eats the guts and liver, and it's hard to type under the hard stuff."

"When you wake up in the morning after a night of drinking white wine, it doesn't leave you feeling like you swallowed wet turds.

"The way I see it," Hank said, "I'm 57 and I've proven that I can drink as long and as hard as the next man. I think that the time comes when the long ignored body asks for a bit of kindness. It has waited around a long time at my door."

Hank was partly responsible for my cutting back on hard liquor, and I began spending less time in bars and more time on my writing.

When I wrote Hank and asked him why he was so down on the San Francisco poets, he said:

"I prefer the fishermen and the corner newsboys. I don't know where people ever got the idea that poetry is a holy thing. I think that the only time poetry gets any good is when it forgets its holiness."

Hank felt Ezra Pound had made the mistake of making a temple and sanctuary out of poetry, and believed Walt Whitman had it backwards when he said, "To have great poetry we must have great audiences." I expressed my pleasure that at long last he had found a good woman to see him through the long nights. He had just returned from Los Alamitos, California, where he had given a reading, and had lost a $469 camera in a taxi. He said the cabbie had recognized him and said, "Hey, you're Charles Bukowski, aren't you?"

Hank denied he was Charles Bukowski and the two women he was with backed him up. He guessed the cabbie was taking some good photos with his new-found luck. He said that after the reading he had fallen down drunk several times: off of planks, out of van doors, into the street, and was limping on a bad right leg. But the poems were still running off his typewriter and he was blessed with the company of Linda.

"I was due for some good luck. She is a stayer with gentle courage and she doesn't play man against man as if she were a golden cow."

Hank still hated giving poetry readings but accepted a reading at The Troubadour. The reading was given to a standing-room only audience, proving he had reached the status of a cult hero. In later years the readings became fewer, even though he had the drawing power of a rock star. In the meantime, lesser poets kept knocking on his door wanting a piece of him, a piece of the action that was missing in their own lives.

Hank's book *Women* was published. He said I would recognize many of the women in the book. He said he wrote it as a "high-low comedy," and believed he came off worse than most of the characters in the book.

"They're only going to think about how I pictured them," he said.

He went on to say he kept drawing madwomen to him like "flies to shit," and that on re-reading *Women* he felt he must have been crazy all those years through 1977.

"Like Thomas Wolfe, after this one, I can't go home again," he said.

By 1978 his translated work was selling well in Germany and France. Someone had written from Sweden and said he was working on a translation of his work. Hank said the guy claimed to be a janitor, which was all right by him, but at that distance it was hard to tell if one was working with a professional or a nut. Hank was writing up to a hundred poems a month but had been lax on writing short stories, except for one Martin had put into book form. He ended his letter by telling me he was scheduled to travel to Germany and France for a month.

In a large way Hank owes his success to John Martin, publisher of Black Sparrow Press. Martin's first four publications were Bukowski broadsides published in early 1966, small limited editions signed by Bukowski. These may be the first Bukowski efforts to bring him royalties. Martin is partly responsible for saving Hank from the further drudgery of those long, killing years at the post office, although I have heard from reliable sources that Hank had a small amount of money saved along with his pension from the post office. If true, he couldn't have been entirely dependent on the small monthly stipend Martin provided. Whatever the case, he soon became the number one writer in the Black Sparrow stable.

Some of Bukowski's friends urged him to look for a larger publishing house. But Hank said it was Martin who had picked him up early and gave him a chance when nobody else would.

"I can't forget this and I won't. He's my publisher. I've got a hound dog loyalty, and I don't mind. It feels good."

Of course Martin too benefited from Bukowski, who was and remains (even after his death) the wild card in Black Sparrow's deck of cards. Bukowski's success made it possible for Martin to become a well-known publisher, not just another small press publisher scratching to survive. Hank could be successful without Martin, but Martin might not be what he is today without Hank. My only complaint with Martin is that, like Colonel Parker, he jealously guarded Hank like a piece of personal property.

In 1980 Benno Kasmayer, publisher of MaroVerlag (a small German publishing house), and Rainer Wehlen, his translator, met with me at a bar in San Francisco, where we shared a few beers. During their visit we discussed the purchase of the German rights for *Second Coming*'s 1974 Charles Bukowski issue. The two Germans had earlier met with Hank and John Martin during their trip to the states. Benno informed me in a July 1983 letter that he had decided to publish a book focusing on Hank's life "as a human being" as opposed to his media image. Earlier Benno had published Hank's book *Shakespeare* in Germany after a large German publisher had turned it down, thereby putting him on favorable terms with Bukowski.

Benno's intention was to publish a book consisting of material which had appeared in the *Second Coming* Bukowski issue. He also wanted to use a short story, "You Kissed Lilly" with drawings previously published in a limited edition by John Martin, who had given permission to re-publish it. Benno believed the story was central to the book. He wanted to add newspaper clippings to illustrate the importance of Bukowski's real life to the central theme of his work. It was Benno's further intention to include "Your Typical Day," a series of screen paintings in five colors to which Hank gave his blessing as part of the book project.

Benno also wanted to use selected photographs and an interview with Hank which had earlier appeared in the *Los Angeles Times*. The book was given the simple title *Buk*. I agreed to sell the German rights for a small advance against 5% royalties, and Wehlen began his work on the German translation. What followed was a debacle of hellish proportions. On July 24, 1983, I received a letter from Wehlen telling me the translation had been completed. But John Martin told Benno he couldn't use the "Lilly" story as part of the book. Martin further said "Winans is not allowed to have foreign rights of texts of Bukowski at his disposal." Martin also withdrew his permission to use any texts of Bukowski, including letters which had previously appeared in the *Second Coming* Bukowski issue. Wehlen said he believed Martin had convinced Hank it was not in his best interest to have the book published in Germany. (This was later confirmed in a telephone conversation I had with Martin.)

Martin said it was counter-productive for Hank to talk about old controversies. This presented a major problem for Benno. The work was already completed and ready to go. Wehlen advised Benno to go ahead with the book since Hank had given his permission to me in two separate letters. Wehlen ended his letter saying the book now consisted of approximately 60% *Second Coming* material and the remainder the "You Kissed Lilly" story, and Hank's description of a "typical day in the life of Bukowski."

I smelled trouble brewing and wrote Hank a letter, asking why he was going back on his word. I quoted from his two letters giving us permission to publish the book, but Hank failed to respond. Benno would also write Hank, but he too failed to receive a reply. Martin's position was that he had given Benno permission to use the story nearly three years earlier, and the long delay in publishing negated any agreement between them. In his letter to Hank, Benno said he was shocked that "a man's word meant so little."

What was the real reason Martin wanted to prevent Benno from publishing the book? It was plain and simple. Hanser-Verlag had paid a considerable sum of money for the German rights to *Ham on Rye* ($50,000), and didn't want another Bukowski book published in the same year, even by a small press.

Benno wrote Bukowski: "You know how I worked my ass off and had to scrape the bottom of the barrel ten years ago to get you out here to Germany. I simply can't understand that big business now wants to make life hard for me, or even impossible."

The old Bukowski would have rallied to Benno's defense, but this was not the Hank of old. Fifty-thousand dollars obviously spoke louder than words.

I wrote Carl Weissner and asked him to intervene. Again I wrote Hank, pointing out that in his letter of April 22, 1982, he had given permission to have Benno go ahead with the book. He had also given his blessing to the project in a subsequent letter dated April 29, 1982. I knew the material in the Bukowski issue had been published prior to the change in the copyright laws and that the material belonged to *Second Coming*. But it was Hank's going back on his word that upset me. I wrote Martin and told him I paid Hank for *He Beats His Women* and it could be considered a commissioned piece of work belonging to the copyright holder, which was *Second Coming*. I quoted from Hank's two letters to me:

"Yeah, Benno and his buddy really suck the beer down. Tough Germans. But good souls. If Benno wants to run the *Second Coming* of Bukowski special issue in German, fine. The way I see it the material is yours. You printed it first."

I pointed out Hank's remarks in a second letter, "Whatever Benno wants. If it works for you, fine."

There was little question that Hank clearly gave permission to go ahead with the publication of Benno's book. This was later confirmed by Bay Area Lawyers For the Arts who, in a written opinion, said the new copyright laws had not gone into effect until 1978. I therefore did not need the permission of either Martin or Hank, as the copyright belonged to *Second Coming*.

On August 3, 1983, Martin told Benno he had published the "Lilly" story in Hank's book *Hot Water Music* and the rights had subsequently been sold to a large German publishing house. Martin concluded his letter to Benno by saying:

"To include any original material by Bukowski in your anthology implies Bukowski approves of the contents, when the fact is he does not care for most of the material in the Bukowski issue of *Second Coming* and thus does not want to be associated with its publication in Germany."

I found this a strange statement. Hank not only gave approval for the publication of the material but on several occasions openly praised the special Bukowski issue of *Second Coming*.

The battle of wills went on for several months, with Martin insisting we needed a signed legal contract from Hank, and that Hank's letters giving his permission were not legally binding. I knew this was not the case. This was a power game, and Martin had both time and money on his side. He held the trump card: when the Special Charles Bukowski issue was published, it bore only the copyright symbol for U.S. rights, not foreign rights.

Eventually a compromise was worked out after Martin accomplished what he had set out to do. That was to delay the Benno book until after the major German publishing house came out with Bukowski's *Ham on Rye*. Money talks!

My only disappointment is that Hank went back on his word. I was even more disappointed to learn he told Martin he hadn't understood what he was giving his permission for, and believed the Benno book was "some kind of domestic project." Surely he had to know that a book published in Germany, in German, was not a domestic project. The whole affair soured me on what success can do to a person. I thought back to the days when I was employed by the San Francisco Art Commission's Neighborhood Arts Program, assigned to work out of the South of Market Cultural Center.

The Sex Pistols came to town, trying to secure a site for their first appearance since the death of their lead singer, Sid Vicious. The Sex Pistols did not want to go through Bill Graham Productions and tried to promote the event on their own. This is something you didn't do when Bill Graham was alive and the reigning power broker of music.

The band found itself with no place to perform. In desperation they came to the South of Market Cultural Center and offered us $1,000 for letting them perform a one-set act. It was a dream come true. We signed a contract with the group's manager, put out publicity flyers, and notified the media. The night was to be a dress rehearsal for the band to try out new material. There would be no introduction or warm-up group.

The crowd was predominately young and noisy. A large number represented the punk rock community. Another large number were attending out of curiosity. Unlike in the past, the fans were not aggressive. Most had come to see Johnny Rotten, the most notorious member of the band since the suicide of Sid. London may be the birthplace of punk rock, but San Francisco was a good surrogate mother. If Johnny Rotten was expecting a rowdy and inebriated crowd, he was disappointed. Every precaution was taken to see that no one brought alcohol onto the premises. The Sex Pistols would come and go with little fanfare, given the circumstances.

The night The Sex Pistols performed the building was packed to capacity. Fifteen minutes before they took the stage, the police brass and a Captain from the Fire Department unexpectedly showed up. We were informed the concert couldn't go on since we lacked a proper permit and the building was a fire hazard. We were asked to go onstage and announce the concert was being canceled. I looked at the crowd and told the police officer that if he wanted a riot on his hands, he could address the crowd himself. There followed a long conference and several hurried telephone calls before the police and fire department officials worked out a compromise. The fire department agreed to station a fire truck outside the building. The police agreed to periodically patrol the outside perimeter. The concert went on as scheduled.

The next day the police showed up at the Cultural Center and confiscated the gate receipts, saying we held an illegal concert without securing the required permits. The money was put into the Mayor's

General Fund. You can't beat the politicians.

I later heard rumors that Bill Graham had turned us in to the police and fire authorities in an attempt to have the concert canceled. I assume the message was you don't perform in San Francisco without going through Bill Graham. "Bill Graham Presents" was and remains today a success story in the music industry. Graham was a giant showman, staging mind-boggling concerts. He also had a giant ego; an ego that demanded he be the kingpin of the music industry. He maintained his status until the day he died in a helicopter crash in 1992. In 1993 he received the American Music Award posthumously for lifetime achievement.

Not long after the incident at the South of Market Cultural Center, I ran into Graham outside City Hall. I approached him and asked if the rumors were true he had turned us in to the police and fire department. He avoided looking at me and said, "Why would I do that?" I said all he had to do was say no. His response: "I'm not going to honor that with a reply." I think that said it all.

Later, I thought perhaps Martin believed he was in the right when he tried to stop the publication of the Benno book, but in March 1988, I changed my mind. It seems Martin (not unlike Bill Graham) believed he owned exclusive rights to Hank.

In a March 3, 1986 letter Hank apologized to Kurt Nimmo, a small press publisher, for a bad experience he had with Martin that closely rivaled my own. Nimmo had published a small stapled book of Hank's poems, which resulted in Martin's subjecting him to the same heavy-handed tactics Benno and I had earlier experienced. In his letter to Nimmo, Hank said it drove Martin to near madness to have another person publish (without his permission) a book of his poems, even if the small book in question was only a limited edition primarily distributed free to Nimmo's friends and subscribers.

Hank said, "Martin has thousands of my poems, a build-up of twenty years of sending him work. He could run off five or six or seven books of my poetry without any problem." Hank went on to accuse Martin of deliberately holding off on the publication of his next book in order to drive up demand. He told Nimmo that Martin talked about how Colonel Parker handled Elvis Presley, holding back Presley's stuff to make the public clamor for him. Hank said he and Martin started off together and that he owed Martin some loyalty. On

151

the other hand, Martin might not "even be in the game now if it weren't for me."

Hank couldn't understand why Martin had called Nimmo on the telephone (as he had done with me), after having already written him a letter. What Martin said to Nimmo isn't discussed, but in his letter Hank said, "Martin seems over-obsessed with the whole fucking thing." Hank ended by apologizing to Nimmo, and telling him he was sorry Nimmo had been put through the "gates of hell." Hank said, "it's ugly and it's not needed."

Hank remained with Martin until the end. Despite what has been said here, they were good for each other. Despite Martin's obsession for keeping Hank to himself, he did help make it possible for Hank to get away from the post office and the deathly vibes of those stone grey walls.

It made me think back to my years at the San Francisco post office. After reading Hank's book, *Post Office*, I was amazed to find I had met the same assholes and zombies Hank had talked about in his novel. You could transfer Hank to the San Francisco post office and put me in the Los Angeles post office and Hank's book would have read the same. It made me appreciate Hank's loyalty to John Martin and Black Sparrow Press. Martin managed to distribute Hank's books in several foreign countries. The foreign royalties allowed Hank to purchase a home, a BMW, and put away a considerable amount of money (one report is a million dollars) in the bank, something Hank could never have imagined during his early Los Angeles days.

Fourteen

Long before the Bukowski/Martin incident I had been corresponding regularly with Hank and Martin's name had come up on more than
one occasion. When Micheline asked Hank to use his influence to have
Black Sparrow publish one of his books, Hank said he had no power
over Martin. Hank said:

"Micheline, Richmond, and you are closer to the blood source, but
then I'm not an editor or a publisher. I'm the wild card in Martin's
stable."

Hank went on to say that he felt Micheline had it in him to be a
force in literature:

"I love the roll of his lines and his looseness. If only he could get
his stuff down into the ground and get off the bitching piano he could
roll on and out. Maybe he will yet. He's got a lot of bullshit in him,
but he can hammer that gong."

Micheline and I became the closest of friends the last two years
before his death. I published a book of his poems (*Last House in
America*), and was the only U.S. press to publish a collection of his
short stories.

After resigning from the COSMEP Board of Directors, I decided to
remain a dues-paying member, and discussed this with Hank in a
telephone conversation. Hank tried to persuade me to break free of all
organizational ties.

"Piss on them," were his exact words.

Hank laughed when I told him a story about how I had done just
that at the 1976 COSMEP Conference, held on the East Coast. I had
been drinking the better part of the day and told Len Randolph (Director of the NEA Literature Program) that he should drive the ill-fated
NEA-financed COSMEP book van off a cliff. To show my contempt
for the project, I took a piss on the back of the van while Randolph
watched in amazement. Harry Smith of *The Smith* later described my
baptism of the van as the "last real act of DA DA."

I later met in private with Randolph and told him the whole grant system was corrupt. Harry Smith, Diane Kruchkow, myself and others favored doing away with grants and establishing a lottery system, or the government could purchase books and magazines from small presses and place them free in hospitals, convalescent homes, schools, prisons and other institutions. Harry, Diane and I also favored replacing the corrupt individual writing grants with a similar lottery system. Many people in the literary community laughed at the proposal, but it would have been fairer than the existing corrupt practices of the NEA.

So corrupt was the system that one year the NEA awarded writing grants to Allen Ginsberg, his lover, several husband and wife teams, and the daughter of a nationally recognized poet. In an attempt to minimize criticism, Randolph and his handpicked literature panel used the wives' maiden names. But it didn't fool those of us who had been tracking the practices of the NEA for several years.

Michael Mooney, novelist and former editor at the *Saturday Evening Post,* took up the cause and wrote a book titled *Ministry of Culture* which detailed the abuses of the NEA Literature Program. But no meaningful changes came about. Mooney related that he had been escorted on a tour of the NEA offices by Mary MacArthur, who showed him box after box of NEA grant requests stacked outside her door, complaining that there were 4,000 or more boxes of manuscripts that needed reading. Mooney said:

"Well I've seen piles like that. I've seen that many, more or less, in the reception room of the editorial floor at Random House. Here I was being told that the entire apparatus of NEA's Literature Program consisted of dealing with manuscripts. What whacked me out was what else would it deal with?"

Mooney said he was unable to make any sense of what was going on at the NEA. He asked John Leonard, a former Director of the NEA Literature Program, how the panel actually went about judging writer's manuscripts. Leonard informed Mooney that writers did not always submit their "best" work for review, so experienced panel members often awarded fellowships based on what they knew the writer *could* do, not the grant application itself.

"Amazing," said Mooney, "the readings made no difference at all."

He further felt Randolph's system of patronage had nothing at all to do with literature.

"The point to Randolph's years was political, first and above all.

What the NEA decided, or didn't decide, about fellowships, presses, magazines, or anything else, did not make one whit's difference. Panels were constituted, voted, collapsed, ad hoc. The secrecy of the panels meant the panels themselves could never know what they themselves had decided. If a panel said no to an application to the NEA, it didn't matter! Randolph could simply arrange the same circumstances for the grantee under some other jurisdiction. The Department of Education, State Art Councils, Foundations, Universities, print centers, what did it matter?"

I knew this to be true. When I first started publishing, Randolph took a liking to me and urged me to submit a grant request to publish two former San Quentin poets (Gene Fowler and William Wantling) whose work Randolph liked. I told Randolph I didn't meet the NEA guidelines, which required a grant applicant to have previously published a minimum of two books.

"Let me worry about that," Randolph said.

I proceeded with the grant request and was soon awarded a two thousand dollar grant for publication of the two books in question.

Congressional hearings were eventually convened to look into the abuses of the NEA literature Program. A committee report was issued which was highly critical of NEA practices. It is hardly surprising these recommendations were never acted upon. I was warned that having Randolph removed as Literature Program Director could result in an even greater evil. This prophecy of doom was fulfilled when David Wilk was appointed as the new Director of the NEA Literature Program, and the ambitious Mary MacArthur (who would later succeed Wilk) as the Assistant Director. The abuse of power continued. Nothing but the names had changed.

This was one of the factors leading to my resignation from the COSMEP Board of Directors. It wasn't just the NEA and the COSMEP board, but also parts of a transcript I came across from the 1950 Nobel Prize ceremonies, where William Faulkner said:

"I believe that man will not merely endure, he will prevail. He is immortal, not because he alone among creatures has an inexhaustible voice, but because he has a soul, a spirit, capable of compassion and sacrifice and endurance.

"The poet's, the writer's duty, is to write about these things. It is his privilege to help man endure by lifting his heart, by reminding him of courage and honor and hope and pride and compassion and pity. The poet's voice need not merely be the record of man. It can be one of the props to help him endure and prevail."

After reading Faulkner's statement, I knew I could no longer remain on the COSMEP Board of Directors. That my decision was the right one was confirmed two months later, when I received a letter from Gordon Kirkwood Yates, a participant in the Folsom Prison Writer's Workshop. I quote from his letter:

"Dear. A.D. It was a good workshop Thursday. You contributed heavily to that fact. Thank you. You have always (to my observance) written and read your work with an enviable professional skill, but yesterday's session was by far the best I've heard.

"I think you're right, getting out of COSMEP was good for you. It seems to have freed you, or, something has, you seem to be enjoying yourself. I'm glad, whatever the reason. In the roughly four years that I've been listening to you read, to my mind you have delivered, almost with a sense of duty (not unlike Bukowski, but quite unlike Bukowski).

"It was always good. Yesterday, that sense of duty, pressure or strain, or whatever, was gone and it was great."

With COSMEP and the NEA divorced from my system, I received a letter from Hank saying he was for the first time having problems with Linda Lee.

"I'm still writing poems and fighting with Linda Lee. Since she's thirty-four, I'm giving away twenty-three years, but I'm right on in there."

Like Bukowski I enjoyed going to the races, although I didn't go to the track as often as Hank did. Hank explained his system in a 1978 letter to Carl Weissner:

"I will rate each horse in 5 categories and he will have numbers, say like this: 2, 7, 4, 3, 6, each contains a meaning, a compilation on the final odds of the horse, the first number must be lower than the odds, the center 3 less than the odds, and the last number near or below the odds, all depending upon the first flash of the tote board and the last."

When I first started going to the track, I used everything from tips to racetrack tout sheets to analyzing the tracking of a particular horse over a long period of time, on dirt and on grass. Nothing had worked! I finally decided to bet only on longshot horses with names I liked.

Horses like Ike's Jeep that came in and paid at l00-1. It wasn't a good system, but I won more often than when I tried to handicap the races. After losing all nine races on the program one afternoon, I returned home and wrote a poem, which I mailed to Hank.

> **Sixteen years high**
> **On this hill**
> **On Laidley street**
> **Writing these words**
> **And drinking**
> **The hard stuff**
> **Playing the horses**
> **Waiting on the big score**
> **And sometimes it's steak**
> **And eggs**
> **But most of the time**
> **It's hamburger helper**
> **And noodles**
> **Waiting for the**
> **Daily Double to come in**
> **At Golden Gate fields**
> **Waiting on the big score**
> **Waiting on the American dream**
> **And after another day of losing**
> **It's back to Gino and Carlo's bar**
> **Eyeing the daily scratch sheet**
> **Looking at the early morning line**
> **Feeling like Bukowski**
> **Keeping an angry eye out**
> **For the poets**
> **Who line-up like**
> **A bad nightmare**
> **At Bay Meadows**
>
> **My eyes scanning the sheet**
> **Looking for the big kill**
> **Silky Sullivan**
> **l6 lengths back**
> **Making his move**
> **Down the back stretch**

All those sad lonely faces
Coming to life
Moving briskly toward
The winner's circle
A matinee idol's dream
Come true

My life on the line
Like a long row
Of hot dogs moving
Down that long line
At the butcher factory
Waiting on the big score
The crowd yelling wildly
Silky Sullivan racing across
The finish line
Declared the winner by a nose
The tote board lighting up
Like a Christmas tree
And then the announcer says:
LADIES AND GENTLEMEN
Please hold on to your tickets
An official inquiry
Has been made
And then it's official
A disqualification for bumping
In the stretch
Silky Sullivan is moved from
First to last

Hypnotic Agent is second
Perverse Fantasy is declared
The winner
And it's back to Gino and
Carlo's bar again
The big score no more
Left feeling like a man
Going to bed with Madonna
And waking up in the morning
Next to Barbara Bush

In July 1978, Hank told me about an interview he gave to *Playboy* during a trip to Germany. He said he was drunk at the time of the interview, and not understanding or speaking German, had no idea what he told the interviewer. He said the interview took place during a two-day drunk. He was paid $650 for his trouble, which helped take some of the edge off the blackout.

Hank's story reminded me of our telephone conversation in which he talked about an interview at a French television station. Hank found the interviewer boring, and when he the kept asking "stupid" questions, Hank walked over to the startled host, rubbed his (bald) head, and walked out of the studio. His story conflicts with another person's who said Hank appeared on a Paris television show hosted by Bernard Pivot; a show viewed by millions of people, where authors are interviewed and asked serious questions. I was informed Hank was drunk and found many of the questions difficult to answer. He finally ripped off the microphone and walked off the stage. Things like this have happened on American television, but more often with actors than authors. Did Hank actually rub the head of the television host? And does it really matter? Fact or fiction, it makes for an interesting story. It's almost certain Hank knew his behavior would gain him more notoriety than if he had stayed and answered questions he found offensive or difficult.

But getting back to Hank's letter. He had experienced a bad evening; his left arm had tightened up and hurt considerably, with pain radiating from thumb to elbow:

"No sleep. No great thoughts. They just send you pain and then it sits on you. Most people say mental pain is the worst, but at least you can fight your way out of it; the other way you depend on outside sources and they may be wrong. I thought in terms of stroke but today the doctor said it was a nerve-ending fuck-up generated by the spine. Now that's not so bad except that I drank three bottles of wine and it didn't ease a thing."

Hank asked when I planned to pay him a visit and talked about what to expect.

"Don't ask me to go to a reading. I might even pick you up at the airport, but can't drive when I've been drinking. Just off a drunk driving rap earlier in the year. I'm on probation and have to be careful. It's almost like the march to the gallows. You know all about this sort of thing."

As Hank continued on his road to fame, he told me: "Jesus, Me and Rod McKuen. Someday I'll be writing you, A.D., and saying that me, Rod and James Dickey went fishing in the Catskills. Then you can attack me and I'll understand."

I told Hank I was growing tired of the power plays of the San Francisco "in-group" poets. He said:

"Don't feel down. Just be glad you aren't them. Greed, envy and stupidity. The infantile gnats want to get on a program with a name and one reason is the gate cut. The other reason is that they think they are going to get up there and, comparatively speaking, they think they are going to be discovered as the real thing. They just don't realize how bad they are; neither do the mothers, wives and girlfriends who support them."

He said he was "heavy into writing" and doing as many as one hundred poems a month. That's a staggering amount of work, even for someone as prolific as Bukowski. He also talked about completing a drunk driving course, which only served to bring back unpleasant memories of my own two DUI arrests.

Fifteen

As Hank's success grew he began learning the business end of publishing. In a 1988 letter to Carl Weissner, he said that, after reading an early City Lights Publishing House contract, he crossed out the 50% payment Ferlinghetti took for foreign sales of Hank's books and wrote in 25%, which was the standard. He told Weissner he wrote Nancy Peters at City Lights Publishing, and learned Ferlinghetti owed him at least $4,500 in royalties. Hank said the change from 50% to 25% would make a big difference in the amount City Lights owed him from sales in France, Italy, Germany and Sweden.

In one of his letters, Hank said that Micheline paid him an unexpected visit and brought "a stack of paintings and poems." Hank said he let Micheline sleep on the sofa. Guessing Micheline might throw up, he placed a wastebasket near Micheline's head.

"You gotta puke, puke in the wastebasket," Hank instructed Micheline.

Hank got up early to drive Micheline to the airport to catch his plane back to San Francisco. Upon his return he found Micheline had missed the wastebasket and wiped up his vomit with a magazine Hank had been published in.

Hank told me, "You ever come to L.A., baby, you hit the basket."

Hank was now busy working on his screenplay *Barfly*. He said it was not an easy thing to do, and this would be his first and last try at writing a screenplay. In August 1979, he wrote to apologize for not writing more often. He was caught up in the usual "troubles and madness" of life, and promised to send me a short story for a *Second Coming* all prose/fiction issue.

Hank said, "I'm hiding as usual from everybody. People will eat you up and spit you out. You know this. I don't know how you have stood publishing this long."

The letters between us grew less frequent. In a letter dated April 22, 1980, Hank said he was still trying to hide out from people who were intent on stealing his time and again touched on his favorite topic, women:

"The day has long past for me when I consider a fuck a very important thing. I still get horny, but when I take in the circumstances, the mind, the strain, the price, I say . . . let others have it."

In a subsequent letter, he said he at last had finished his screenplay *Barfly*.

"Five rewrites. It's a little different game from the poetry game. It's something like a series of paintings which keep moving. There's little artistic freedom."

Hank said he would soon be sixty years old, but his health was holding up.

"There's much more typing to be done. The snivelers will be sickened for some time to come, I think."

I recall a late May 1979 telephone conversation. I asked if he would consider reading at a benefit for *Second Coming* and offered him a cut of the gate. Hank said he didn't want to fly to San Francisco, not even for a benefit reading. He complained that everyone was asking him to read even though they knew how he felt, and said he expected more from me. He knew *Second Coming* was having financial problems and wanted to see the magazine survive. He just couldn't bring himself to do another reading, and didn't want to ever set foot in San Francisco again.

I didn't press the issue and don't recall much of what we discussed. He must have had the conversation on his mind, as a few days later a letter arrived in the mail.

"For Christ sake, man. I can't read at a benefit and get paid for it," he said. "Better count my ass out. Besides, I have started another novel, and there won't be many new poems because of this, and there is nothing I hate more than reading the old stuff. Please set me free on this one."

In January 1981, I mailed Hank the latest issue of the magazine and a few Second Coming books he was not aware of. He wrote back and said he was glad I was managing to survive the San Francisco literary scene:

"In my opinion, San Francisco is the worst place for surviving." Hank said he was glad to live in San Pedro, where people could "walk down the street easy like, avoiding trouble and waiting on death without thinking about it too much."

In August 1982 I wrote and asked Hank why I hadn't heard from him in awhile. He said it wasn't me, it was just that he was going through some bad times with Linda Lee:

"She started out as a good woman, but she rapidly changed into something else, especially during the last two years. Maybe it's time for me to retire from the game."

He went on to say it was easier to just drink and listen to symphony music.

"I just need the horses and the booze. The women always want to do something. Well, they can do it with someone else."

Hank commented on the latest issue of *Second Coming*:

"Jesus, you're still at it. The mag, the anthologies, the books. Don't kid me, you've got to have a taste for this sort of thing. I thought you were going to dump it and get more into your own writing. You might yet."

Hank said that while women might be draining his lifeblood, his luck with writing was still good.

"There are moments when it runs flat, when the old joy and exploration is gone, and I think, well, you're 62, the women don't want you and the typer doesn't either. Then one night I'm at the machine and it all comes roaring out and I feel normal again."

In those days I didn't keep copies of my letters to Hank or anyone else. But on February 17, 1983, while working the midnight shift at Saint Francis Memorial Hospital, I wrote Hank a letter. For some reason, I made a xerox copy.

Hello Buk:

Received your letter today and thanks for sending me a check for $20 for two extra copies of the 10 Years In Retrospect Anthology. You'll have the largest chunk of work from the looks of it. It'll be over 200 pages, maybe closer to 240 pages. Well partner, I have finally slowed down with my publishing, only doing one issue of the magazine in '82, and no books. The anthology will come out next year. If I'm still alive in 1984 I'll do one more book and one issue of the magazine. After that *Second Coming* will become irregular. I just don't have the energy anymore.

This security job at the hospital is killing me. I'll try and save

some money and stick it out one more year. It's such a drag. I can't sleep during the day and all I see at night is death coming and going through the hospital doors.

The supervisors are real shits and I know they'd like to get rid of me. They have people on my own shift spying on me, and I think the head of security is involved in drugs. To answer your question on whether I'll ever be able to get out of publishing, I don't honestly know. I admit it's burrowed its way into my veins and taken over my blood. But not quite as bad as it was in the past. I mean I have quit the senseless and time-consuming political shit with the likes of the National Endowment For the Arts people, whose vibes lie somewhere between a burned out lightbulb and the Cafe Trieste North Beach poets crowd.

No amigo, I'm not drinking eggnogs with Harold Norse and the gang. You say Neeli has hung around with Ferlinghetti too long, but I guess that's in part due to his doing a biography on him. There are worse people to hang around with.

Micheline was going to Denver, the last I heard, but shit, he was in Europe not long ago, and I haven't been in contact with him for some time. Jack calls when he needs more copies of his book, or to bend my ear with how bad the world treats poets, but I still love the bastard. Maybe he'll take up residence in Germany, or a kinder country that will give him his due. He does have a raw talent, more than many of the Beats who gained media attention.

Micheline and Ferlinghetti are still feuding, both creating with the paintbrush, at the moment. Both wanting recognition too. I guess poetry isn't enough for them.

Jack's paintings have a certain childish appeal to them. When I think of Ferlinghetti, I think back to the time when he posed with that Russian poet in front of Carol Doda's, her large billboard breasts in the background. Hardly a revolutionary image. Is this what the Beats have come to? I think Kerouac might spit in the face of the whole gang, if he were alive and forced to see the happenings going on at Naropa.

Ferlinghetti calls you the "author of the future." Coming from a poet of the past, I guess that's praise. I guess I've ranted enough. You're right about what you say about women. I get lucky and get laid every now and then, but I'm not into the day-to-day entertainment it demands. You're right about their always wanting to go somewhere and do something. I'll try to make it out your way this summer and share a few drinks with you.

I've never been to San Pedro. I always pictured it as a small Japanese fishing village. Don't worry, I won't give out your latest unlisted telephone number. I know how it is to have your phone number in the hands of someone you don't want to have anything to do with.

Let me close by saying I enjoyed your latest book immensely. It may be your best book to date. Funny how two people experience the same things growing up. We have more in common than I first thought. Well, it was a good read. I just wanted to let you know.

Take care of yourself and drop a line whenever the mood hits you. It's always good to hear from you. I want you to know that I don't sell your letters, or write you with the intention of hoarding your letters with the purpose of selling them later on, nor have I been keeping copies of my letters to you. I find that putting a carbon in the typewriter takes away from the personal tone of the letter. There exists no complete exchange of letters between us (or anyone else) and that's the way I want it.

It's getting close to the end of the shift and a nurse is knocking on the door. I wish she were coming to offer me her body, but she only wants me to put away a patient's valuables in the office safe. Got to go. Hang in there.

A. D.

Hank seemed moved by my letter, and talked about my commitment to editing and publishing.

"I shouldn't push you too much about your editing. I mean knock it too much, because you and *Wormwood Review* have published the best stuff around, and you've got a good eye for the typed page."

I unburdened my soul, again telling him how depressing I found the job; all those people lined up, waiting on death, coughing and spitting up their insides. Nurses with dollar bill eyes, strutting their stuff into the parking lot after a long night's work; too tired to laugh, overcome with failure and fatigue. And the doctors, so sad they couldn't be God, hiding their failures in cocktail glasses or between the legs of the angels of mercy. Hank responded with a telephone call.

"God Damn it, you've got a poem there. It's right there in your letter screaming to be told. All you need is to put in the proper line breaks."

We talked about the possibility of my writing a book about my hospital experiences, and whether it should be fiction or non-fiction.

"I did it with the post office," Hank said, "and you can do it with the hospital."

The book never became a reality, but my discussion with Hank did result in a long hospital poem that would later be published. In our letters I filled Hank in on the local literary gossip, which was something he seemed to enjoy. When time passed and I hadn't followed up on my promise to visit him, he telephoned and said:

"Your time is running out, man. I'm not getting any younger. You get your ass down here and we'll have one last drinking bout to talk about."

I asked him how he felt about the Beats. He said he found Allen Ginsberg to be a "nice enough guy," but turned down his invitation to visit the Naropa institute because he wasn't into that sort of thing.

"I never liked the Beats. They were too self-promotional, and the drugs gave them all wooden dicks or turned them into cunts. I'm from the old school. I believe in working and living in isolation. Crowds weaken your intent and your originality."

In another conversation, Hank said Neeli Cherkovski had paid him a visit in the company of his aunt. A week later a manuscript arrived in the mail with a request to write a foreword for the book. Hank said he felt Neeli had been in San Francisco too long, and that the manuscript was so bad he had been forced to trash it. Neeli denies this. When I told Hank I was having my own problems with women, he said:

"But Kid, I too have been pissed upon by cement women. The best thing of all is getting away from them for awhile. Shit, man, I'm going to open another bottle of wine. Life is good enough to drink away."

During this time, Hank was making good money writing short stories for men's magazines. In December 1983, he wrote and thanked me for using a photograph of him on the front cover of the *Second Com-*

ing: Ten Years In Retrospect anthology which Hank had generously contributed to.

Hank said that after all these years he decided Linda Lee was the right woman for him. Despite arguments and near breakups, there were no others like her. He ended his letter by saying:

"Linda says I still look the same except for the hair. It has some silver. I hope I don't look the same or write the same either. O.K. Duck and make sure you hide low."

Sixteen

When I complained about the disadvantages of working the hospital graveyard shift, Hank was not overly sympathetic.

"Sounds like you've got a work load, and that graveyard shift can do funny things to the mind, but it beats daylight work. And a good man can still find time to do a few good things if some woman isn't driving him crazy. You're a good man, hold on."

I wasn't convinced! Night after night I was called to assist in clearing the ambulance entrance for the never-ending convoy arriving with flashing lights and screaming sirens, and was frequently asked to assist in wheeling heart attack victims into the ER. I don't recall too many surviving that ride. I thought it was a bad omen when the morgue attendant administered CPR while the ER doctor and nurses stood around talking. The worst part of the job was not being able to sleep. I barely managed more than four hours on any given night, and my body clock never adjusted.

Hank's letters helped see me through eight years of living hell. A hell far worse than the five years I spent at the post office. Meanwhile, Hank was enjoying his life in San Pedro.

"Hardly a poet in a truck load. I'm left alone here, not only by the poets, but by the ladies."

Hank said Linda Lee was enough for him, but it was nice not to be called upon to service women from the past or, worse yet, those who wanted part of his present or future.

By 1985 I was at a low point. The job at the hospital was becoming unbearable. My best friend had contracted AIDS and I watched him die a slow and terrible death. I had just broken up with a woman for whom I still had strong feelings. To make matters worse, I had been the victim of two burglaries, the second of which resulted in the loss of my typewriter, camera, television set and most of my clothing. After a three-day drinking binge, I wrote Hank a handwritten letter of despair. He responded:

"Jesus Christ, man, your handwriting gets worse and worse. Really hard to read. Have you turned into a total drunk? I hope you're all right. I'm strictly on the wine now, and try not to go to it every night, but I'm dependent, and it's hard for me to write without it. A lot of shit troubles here, and I'm trying to straighten them out."

It was reassuring knowing there was someone who seemed to care and who could share his own problems. I bought a new typewriter and for the most part managed to stay away from the bars. I was not always successful. I had been addicted to alcohol since my teens, even before I enlisted in the military. What was Hank's reaction?

"Yes, the bars finally lose their appeal. I mean the trouble and the fights, the drunk tanks, the women, the stupid bartenders, the bad conversations and the bad music. Those places are just full of lonely people, and I finally decided that I wasn't lonely, not for that."

He talked about the virtue of drinking at home alone, if indeed one had to drink. About not having to worry about being arrested for drunk driving or having your license suspended. I later sent Hank an article I had come across which was critical of his work. He wrote back about the petty envy and vicious attacks directed at him, but was more concerned about the inaccuracies and misquotes in the article.

"I think that one of the best things that ever happened to me was that I was so long unsuccessful as a writer, and had to work for a living until I was fifty years old.

"It kept me away from other writers and their parlor games and their back-stabbing and their bitching, and now that I've had some luck, I still intend to absent myself from them."

I sensed he was still hurting from a slight by Lionel Rolfe, who had published a history of Bohemian writers in Southern California titled *Literary L.A.* While other writers in the anthology were presented in great detail, Hank was given only a brief mention on the last page. The anthology was later updated, and Hank received twelve pages with his photograph featured on the cover.

In early 1985 I began experiencing severe intestinal discomfort, and wrote Hank about the pain. He wrote back:

"Hope your health is getting better. The problem with getting down in your health is that it's usually accompanied by a host of other problems, and that's when each of us finds out how really alone he is."

It was about this time that he was beginning to have his own health problems, but he didn't discuss them with me in any detail.

In the summer of 1985 Hank finally married Linda Lee at a restaurant near San Pedro harbor. When I heard of the marriage I sat down and scrawled a poem on a large postcard, which I'm sure Hank had trouble deciphering. (The poem later appeared in a small magazine published by Steve Richmond.)

Postcard For Charles Bukowski
On Learning Of His Wedding To Linda Lee

Dear Hank
Hope this postcard finds
You well
As for me
It's the usual
Hell
Heard that you married
Linda Lee
Maybe there's still
Hope for me
That must have been
Quite a sight
You dressed in white
Dancing like Zorba
The Greek with
Oriental hostesses
So gentle and meek
Here on the home front
Neeli is still being
Neeli
Ferlinghetti is off
Somewhere in the Nile
Heard that Corso
Is in South Africa
Practicing his
Zeig Heil
And they say Burroughs
May be growing senile

Hear that you're
Sixty-five
Still going to the track
Eating trout
Your enemies dismayed
No doubt
Micheline is still
Looking for a hit man
He would have made
A great WW II
Suicide pilot
For Japan
Me
I'm feeling great
Except for my stomach
Which is walking
An eight story
Fire escape
Intestines chewing away
At fast food gourmet
But the drinking helps
See me through the day
Booze words and
An occasional lay
Beats the hell out
Of politics and
The likes of Mao
And Che

Still reading your work
At every chance I get
Happy to see that
You still have the power
To make me gasp for air.
Well pard
My hand is getting cramped
And I'm running out of space
Gone on far too long

Like an old Sinatra song
So I'll just end it here
With this good cheer
And promise to keep it down
To once or twice
A year

I asked Hank to send me a photo of his wedding for use in a future issue of the magazine, but he declined, saying he appreciated the gesture but there were "forces working against it."

As I approached my 50th birthday, I wrote Hank and asked him for advice about quitting work and devoting my full time to writing, as Hank had done when he quit the post office at forty-nine. His advise:

"I don't know what to tell you. I had to quit my job. My whole body was in pain, and I could no longer lift my arms. They had beat on my body and mind for decades. And I didn't have a dime. I had to drink it away to free my mind from what was occurring. I decided that I would be better off on skid row. Yeah, I was afraid. I had fear that I could never make it as a writer, moneywise. I just drank and sat at the typewriter. I wrote my first novel, *Post Office,* in nineteen nights. I drank beer and scotch and sat around the apartment in my shorts. I smoked cheap cigars and listened to the radio. I wrote dirty stories for the sex magazines. It got the rent paid, and also got the soft ones and the safe ones to say, 'He hates women.' The poetry readings came and I hated them, but it was more $$$, and I wrote and wrote and wrote. I loved the banging of the typewriter. Sometimes I think it was only the sound of the typer that I wanted.

"It wasn't so much that I was *trying* to be a writer, it was more like doing something that felt good to do. The luck gradually mounted, and I kept on writing, and certain writers began to hate me. That doesn't matter. What matters is that I didn't die on that post office stool."

Hank said if I wanted to quit work, I might want to consider working five hours a day. He felt a part-time job wasn't that bad and wouldn't kill a man, while still leaving enough time to write. In closing, he said:

"If any of this gives light to what you're trying to do, trying to escape from, good. I think that any gamble beats sitting still when the intolerable walls close in."

Needing a feeling of security, I remained at Saint Francis Hospital and occasionally tried my hand at the men's magazine market. But things had changed since I sold short stories to *Easy Rider* and *Berkeley Barb.* In September 1985, Hank wrote and said if I still wanted to visit him, this might be a good time. He expected the shooting of his screenplay *Barfly* to be completed soon. I had been promising to visit for a long time, but something always came up to prevent it.

In January 1986 I was surprised to receive a letter from him just days before my 50th birthday.

"The big fifty is something. Once you get there you can handle most anything. After fifty, it's like each year is a free one to play with. It's a great feeling. The older you get the more you learn how to duck shit you wouldn't have ducked before. It gives you time for the essentials. And one of the essentials is not letting other people waste your life."

He related a series of horror stories he experienced with the men's magazines, which he claimed had stiffed him. One of the editors owed him a large amount of money and had no intention of paying.

"I thought I'd warn you about this because if you're thinking about freelancing, you'll need to find some reliable markets."

Hank seldom wrote political poems or discussed politics, so I was surprised when I received his letter praising my book *The Reagan Psalms,* a biting satire about the Reagan Administration. Hank said:

"This is one of the most sickening times in our history. The poor whites pitted against the blacks. All those gains made in the last half century, Al, they have been lost back to this smiling oaf, Ronnie. Christ, I seldom get this way about politics, but it's all so obvious. Let me puke."

Hank seemed amused that Studs Terkel read portions of the book over his Chicago radio station. But he strongly believed my time would be better spent writing poetry or a novel.

Following yet another period of silence, Hank sent me a short letter. "Yes, I know that I haven't written you many letters of late. My life has taken on nightmarish proportions. It seems like any move that I make is the wrong one. Somebody's crazy, and it could be me. You've been around a long time, and you seem to have held it together. Be careful, old buddy, on any moves you make."

In the early summer of 1986 I mailed Hank contributor copies of Volume Fourteen, Number 1 of *Second Coming* magazine. The issue was dedicated to the late black Beat poet, Bob Kaufman, who even today remains a legend in North Beach and France.

Kaufman came to San Francisco in 1953 after working as a merchant seaman. Following World War Two he became involved in union work, hanging around with people from the political left. Before traveling to San Francisco, he hung out with the Greenwich Village Beats, whose neighborhood was similar to North Beach in the 50's. Kaufman was a giant among surrealist poets, and his imagery was more profound (and humorous) than some other Beat poets who later gained fame: Ginsberg, Corso, Ferlinghetti, LeRoi Jones, to name a few.

When I returned home from the military I found North Beach had become a thriving Bohemian colony of creativity. In a six-block area on lower Grant Avenue there were bars, cafes and coffeehouses filled with poets, artists and jazz musicians. While Grant Avenue was the main hub of creativity, it extended to Broadway and Columbus. All the way to the Produce District, where the self-proclaimed King of the Beats, "Big Daddy Nord," held court in an old converted warehouse. The parties at Big Daddy Nord's pad were legendary and went on non-stop, until one evening a young man, stoned on drugs, walked off the roof and killed himself.

But the real action was on Grant Avenue. It was lined with establishments like The Co-Existence Bagel Shop, The Coffee Gallery, the Anxious Asp, The Spaghetti Factory, and The Place, where Jack Spicer and Richard Brautigan hosted "Blabber Mouth Night," where anyone could get up and speak whatever was on their mind. Poets and writers regularly made the trip from San Francisco to New York and back: Ginsberg, Cassady, Kerouac and Corso, among them. Standing out in this crowd was the poet Bob Kaufman.

I first saw him at the Co-Existence Bagel Shop on the corner of Grant and Green. Kaufman was the star attraction. A hipster among the hip. A Black Jesus of the fifties, laughing and carrying on, reciting Lord Buckley in between dynamite readings of his own work. He was dressed in a red corduroy jacket, and looked strikingly handsome in a beret and goatee. He looked more like a Greenwich Village artist than a poet. Later, I saw him at The Place and various North Beach bars, or wandering up and down Grant Avenue, heavy in thought. At the time

I was too insecure to do more than acknowledge him with a passing nod.

Kaufman wasn't like other Beat poets who frequented the beach. He never attempted to push his own literary career. He was an oral poet. If not for his wife Eileen, most of his poetry would be lost. Like me, Kaufman liked T.S. Eliot's "Love Song of J. Alfred Prufrock," and could recite it from memory. He loved jazz, and was friendly with Charlie Parker, Lester Young and Charlie Mingus.

One night I was sitting at Spec's Bar across the street from City Lights, waiting for Eileen Kaufman and a friend. We were going to a party in Palo Alto hosted by Miriam Patchen, widow of Kenneth Patchen. Kaufman entered the bar and began reciting William Blake, T.S. Eliot and other masters he had memorized. I sat in awe and watched him pace back and forth, performing non-stop for nearly an hour. When Eileen and Alix finally arrived and took Kaufman to the party, I stayed behind to write a poem about him. It was later published in a North Beach magazine and hung outside the bar in a glass case until Bob's death in 1986.

Earlier in the 60's I was standing in back of the Coffee Gallery, listening to a poet read, when I felt a hand on my shoulder. I turned and saw the smiling face of Kaufman.

"Are you going to read your work tonight?" he asked.

I hadn't planned on reading and hadn't brought any poems to read. When I told him I didn't have any poems with me, he said, "I came to hear you read."

I drove several miles across town in a torrential rainstorm to pick up my poems, convinced he would be gone by the time I returned. But I found him sitting alone in the back of the room. I read for about twenty minutes, very much aware of his eyes on me. I dedicated the last poem to him. When I finished reading, I discovered he had quietly slipped out of the bar.

It was Kaufman who wrote on the walls of the Co-Existence Bagel Shop, "Adolph Hitler, tired of burning Jews and bored with fucking Eva Braun, moved to North Beach and became a cop."

This remark, and the fact he was dating a white woman, caused police officer William Bigarini to make Kaufman a target of his wrath. Kaufman was frequently arrested and taken downtown to the Hall of Justice, where he was physically abused. Beatings, drugs, physical abuse, and forced shock treatments left him a shadow of the brilliant poet he had once been. There were, however, moments when he showed his former sense of humor. Like the day I was drinking at the old Coffee Gallery, watching Gregory Corso play mind games with a group of young admirers.

Someone asked Corso to name a list of major and minor poets. He quickly named Ginsberg and Corso as major poets, relegating Kaufman and Micheline to minor poet status. Corso wasn't aware that Kaufman was standing near the entrance to the bar. I asked Kaufman to rate Corso. He flashed a smile and said, "major/minor," and left to loud applause.

Kaufman and I had a special relationship that didn't require conversation. Many times when I was stone drunk, I would turn around and find him standing next to me at the bar. We often communicated with our eyes. When we did speak the conversation was often not a lengthy one. I attended his 50th birthday party, and brought the poem I wrote for him at Spec's Bar. I had another party to attend that evening and as the hour grew late, I approached Kaufman and said I wanted to read a poem, but had to leave. Kaufman walked to the front of the room and grabbed the mike and announced, "The next poet is A.D. Winans." That's the kind of relationship we had.

On January 12, 1986 I was celebrating my birthday in North Beach when Shig, the former manager of City Lights, stopped and told me Kaufman had died at the age of sixty, a victim of emphysema. I went from bar to bar informing one friend after another of the tragic news. The reaction was stunned silence followed by the inevitable "Shit" or "God Damn."

The truth is that death is not a good conversation piece.

Q.R. Hand, a poet friend of Kaufman, later told me a story of how he visited Kaufman in the hospital. Kaufman was plugged into tubes and looked terrible. Q.R. leaned over and asked Kaufman if there was anything he could do for him. Kaufman slowly raised himself up from the bed, leaned on one elbow, and said, "I need Bob Kaufman back." The drugs, alcohol abuse, and shock treatments would not allow it. But even in his reduced physical state, he was more the poet than anyone I knew in North Beach, with the possible exception of Jack Micheline.

Kaufman never lost his sense of humor, not even in death. Lynne Wildey, who cared for Kaufman until he went to a convalescent home, visited with him the night he died. Just before she left, Kaufman smiled at her and said, "Drop in the next time you're in the neighborhood."

If Kaufman was not afforded the respect he deserved in his homeland, he was revered in France, where he is considered by many to be the American Rimbaud.

The night of his death I promised myself to pay tribute to him in a special *Second Coming* issue. Kaufman had a way of touching those he met or who read his work, and this was true of Bukowski too. Hank had several of his own poems in the special Kaufman issue, and wrote to tell me:

"Today I picked up the *Second Coming* Kaufman issue. It gave me more than a sad feeling, although I never knew the man. I don't know what trapped him: drugs, booze or leaning too much upon the artist. But let the dead rest. Even if death won't. That's the trouble with death. I think too many of us have it figured like a good night's sleep; whereas in actuality we may never get out of this fucking fire."

The shame is Kaufman's peers did little to make sure he received the recognition he deserved. In his letter, Hank said he was trying to cope with problems in his own life.

"When things get fairly dark around here, I think of Dante's last years and realize that I should only show one-tenth the backbone that he did, and there's no problem at all."

In a return letter, I told him I was having trouble coping with how fast life was passing me by. Hank said:

"Time passes by fast here too, though writing isn't a hard job. Not for me. It just comes out. I mean that. I'm 66 years old and haven't much time left, but this doesn't concern me too much. Leaving this earth will not be a wrenching thing to do. The strangest thing to me is that I got so lucky with my writing at such a late age."

Kaufman and Hank were both atheists, and I recall a poem Kaufman wrote about his father drowning when he was only nine years old.

a father, whose mine?
floating on seaweed rugs
to that pearl tomb, shining
beneath my bayou's floor.

dead, and dead,
and you dead too.
tears will wash away
her dirty murdered soul
God will be called on
to atone for his sins.

They gave Kaufman a grand sendoff. At the memorial Ferlinghetti read a letter from Allen Ginsberg, who was in New York and unable to attend. Michael McClure read a poem of Kaufman's. Bob's handsome son Parker (a part-time model) informed the crowd that simultaneous ceremonies were being held in France, New York, Belgium and Germany to coincide with the San Francisco services.

Jack Micheline read a poem for Kaufman outside the church to a large crowd, as a Municipal bus passed with confused passengers peering out the windows.

In North Beach on January 23, 1986, a warm and sunny day, a second memorial service was held for Kaufman. Poets and friends gathered outside the Cafe Trieste, along with Kaufman's son. A Dixieland band accompanied the crowd up Grant Avenue, stopping to play music at each bar Kaufman had frequented. The march ended at Washington Square Park where a few words were spoken. His friends then drove down to the Marina, boarded two boats and scattered his ashes out across the bay.

I would later have a telephone conversation with Hank touching on Kaufman's ashes being scattered at sea. Hank said:

"They can plant me in the ground when my time comes and let the worms have their way with me, but I don't want any morbid vultures coming to my resting place. It's more likely some San Francisco poet will come to piss on my grave. That is, if they have it in them."

Hank said that when his time came he didn't want a eulogy. No priest. Just a few close friends. I told Hank I was still having trouble staying away from the booze. His reply:

"The drinking, it takes more out of me too, but I can't figure any other way around it. When the world closes in too much, the bottle seems the only way to ease things. The body must pay, of course, but the mind has to be considered too."

Hank talked about fame and recognition and what it meant in the long run. He felt the problem was how seriously a poet/writer takes what the media does to him. He believed that the media hyped many people who didn't deserve it in the slightest. Hank felt most poets and writers were too weak and emotional. Too easily seduced by camera, lights, and attention. That when an artist reached a point of being really good, the media realized it had a wild animal, and they fed it to keep it from getting any stronger. Hank said there was a strong link between creativity and adversity. When a writer got strong enough, they simply took away the adversity. He swore this would never happen to him.

On the spur of the moment I decided to drive to San Pedro and pay Hank a surprise visit. But on arriving, I found he wasn't home. When I wrote and told Hank of my disappointment, he said:

"I feel bad about that, but I think you have my telephone number."

I told him I got drunk in North Beach and spent a hundred dollars in the bars. He replied:

"Musta been some bar(s), baby. Best to get some fine stuff and drink alone. That way you know the company is good."

When I told Hank how hangovers were killing my creativity, he said: "Recovering from a drunk myself. Soon will be sixty-seven. I used to be sick just one day afterwards. Now it seems to be two. Well, the booze should have killed me long ago."

In May 1987 Hank wrote to inform me the shooting of *Barfly* had been completed, and was to be shown at the Cannes Film Festival. I tried to imagine him at the beach, on the French Riviera, watching a bevy of topless women parade by.

"I'm not going over there because I feel it has nothing to do with the work," Hank said. "It should be out in the U.S. by the fall. Right now I'm just trying to stay away from the booze, at least at home. Wine will do. However, outside, I sometimes slip off into the vodka and much too much of it."

Barfly starring Mickey Rourke and Faye Dunaway and directed by Barbet Schroeder, hit the movie houses in 1987. Hank was now a cult hero courted by Hollywood movie stars. He would later use this experience to write *Hollywood*, a book focusing on the pitfalls surrounding the making of a small budget movie. Despite this newfound big-time exposure, he remained largely outside the mainstream, not something he necessarily minded.

There were earlier films based on Hank's lifestyle, including *Tales of Ordinary Madness* and *Love Is A Dog From Hell,* a Belgian film based on several of Hank's short stories. These early efforts received mixed reviews, and were attended by small audiences, but were nevertheless important preludes to *Barfly.*

In the last part of 1988 I suffered a severe neck injury that kept me unemployed for nearly two years, and which ultimately led to the demise of *Second Coming.* I was in so much pain that I sent a form letter to my friends (including Hank) telling them until further notice I would not be answering any mail. Hank and I all but stopped writing. I continued to follow his career with interest, and was never bored with what he wrote. And yes, Hank did write that play he had earlier talked about doing. It was called *The Life and Times of Charles Bukowski.*

The last letter I received from Hank was in October 1988. It simply said, "Sorry about your neck problem. Don't let them operate on you except as a last resort. Most operations for neck and back problems only seem to aggravate the problem. I've had a series of maladies all year long. My worst year in some time. How I wrote and finished *Hollywood* I have no idea. But I did it, almost in a haze. All in all, the Gods have been good to me."

Seventeen

Hank's main contribution to poetry was to write in a clear understandable style that appeals to the common man. Tough guy language aside, he showed a style and sensitivity unlike any poet I know.

Now here it was March 1994, and the Gods had called in their marker on the grand old man of literature. Young kids and old poets would soon begin writing their odes. Some would be sincere and some self-serving. Old enemies would get out their knives and sharpen them. Critics would pound their typewriter keys with a new vengeance. The moneymakers would make money. These were some of the thoughts going on inside my head that day in March 1994.

I recalled that Hank and I had appeared together in *Beat Scene Magazine*, a slick literary quarterly published in England. Hank had a poem in the issue titled "Eulogies." The poem spoke about how we can't stand this person when he is alive, but how wonderful he is after he is dead. The poem closed with the following lines:

> **If only at a funeral service**
> **somebody would say**
> **what an odious gathering of cells**
> **that once was**
> **Even at mine**
> **let there be a bit of truth**
> **then the clean**
> **dirt.**

We know this much about Hank's funeral. The memorial service was held at Green Hills Memorial Park, which looks down upon San Pedro and the Los Angeles Harbor. Sean Penn, who became a close friend of Hank's, was in attendance in formal dress. Also attending were Gerald Locklin, a poet-friend; John Martin, Hank's publisher; Carl

Weissner, Hank's German translator; John Thomas, a writer and long-time friend, and a few writers associated with Black Sparrow. Most of the mourners were non-literary friends Hank knew and enjoyed from his neighborhood and San Pedro haunts. The ordinary folk Hank wrote and cared about. I suspect this is what he would have wanted.

Locklin tells us, in an article that appeared in *Sure Magazine*, that the religious rites were conducted by a trio of Buddhist monks and there was a lot of chanting and bowing. I'm sure that Hank wouldn't have been offended, and might even have been amused. Locklin said the monk in charge of the rites spoke from the pulpit in two languages, but it was difficult to understand either of them.

After the memorial service, the crowd left and made its way to the ridge of the hill, where the grave awaited Hank's remains. The ceremony at the gravesite is said to have been brief, with a few people tapping the coffin in what Locklin described as a gesture of good luck.

A few things seem worth mentioning. The casket almost got away from the pallbearers down the hill. One of the monks positioned himself at the grave for a photo opportunity. Sean Penn told Locklin, as the monks chanted around Hank's casket, "Don't they know this is America? Why aren't they speaking Spanish?"

As for Hank, he left us a final book, *Pulp*. It's unlike anything Hank had written. Go out and buy yourself a copy, and when you're through with it, get your butt over to the typewriter, sit down with a glass of white wine, and see if you can write a poem half as good as Hank.

.

Epilogue

It's sometime in the 90's, I think 1991. I run into Neeli Cherkovski, Hank's close friend, when he was known as Neeli Cherry. I accompany Neeli to the home of his lover. It isn't long before the telephone rings. It's Hank on the other end of the line. I can only guess what they're talking about, but it has something to do with Hank's health. I watch Neeli cradle the receiver in his hand. "Don't talk like that," Neeli says. "We all feel sick at times. It happens when you get older."

I ask Neeli to let me speak with Hank but he ignores me, using the telephone extension cord to move away. I ask him two, three more times to let me talk to Hank. Finally, Neeli turns in my direction. "A.D. is here," Neeli tells Hank. "He wants to talk to you."

Neeli seems nervous and tells Hank goodbye, hanging up the telephone. I ask Neeli what Hank said. Neeli looks embarrassed and says, "Hank said that he read your poem about him in a magazine, and said to say 'Fuck You!'"

That was it? He told Neeli to tell me, "Fuck You!" Just because I had written a poem critical of him? A poem that hadn't even mentioned him by name.

Was this the same man that said someday he would go fishing in the Catskills with Rod McKuen and James Dickey, and that when that day came, I could attack him, and he would understand? Was this the same man who had put down more poets in his writing than a baker's dozen of serial critics? Was this the same man who had called sweet Annie a no-talent poet and other obscene things, and when I chastised him for it, laughed and said he didn't understand why she was so upset? Was this the same man who once drank Schlitz beer and kept green tuna in his icebox when he lived in the slums of Los Angeles?

Was this the same man who turned on LouJon, whose only crime was to publish two of Hank's books in the most beautiful manner imaginable? Was this the same man who, when he co-edited *Laugh Literary and Man the Humping Gun,* had rejected the work of William Wantling with a terse, "These poems don't make it and your work was never that good to begin with?"

Bukowski who, when he became rich and famous and heard that *Second Coming* was having financial problems, wrote and sent me ten dollars and told me not to spend it all on beer.

Bukowski, who took delight in tormenting Harold Norse, and who said, "I enjoy my assholeness. I can tear a man in half in a short story," and often did.

Bukowski, who gave Jack Micheline a dollar when he was down and out and said, "Jack wants the golden ring in the sky, but the hardest thing he works is his mouth."

Bukowski, who wrote a vicious poem, "A Serious Fellow," dedicated to Steve Richmond who, at the time, was his best friend.

Bukowski, who gave me permission to sell the German rights to the special Bukowski issue, only to go back on his word.

Bukowski, who told me in a letter, "I never liked the Beats; they were too self-promotional," only to later pal around with Sean Penn and the Hollywood crowd.

Bukowski, who slammed time and time again his once closest friend, Neeli Cherkovski.

I guess Harold Norse was right when he told me not to criticize Bukowski in print, that Bukowski couldn't stand love, that Bukowski couldn't stand the truth, that Bukowski couldn't stand criticism.

Norse, who said in his poem for Bukowski, "Leave him alone. Don't go writing articles and pieces about him forever in the little magazines. It only makes him run off at the mouth. The bad mouth. Attacking his friends. Attacking his well wishers. Leave him alone. He will never accept you. He will betray you. He will piss on you, belittle and destroy you. And the worst thing you can say is I love you."

Well, I love you, Buk. Wherever you are. Despite your many faults. I love your work. Oh how I love your work.

I loved you far more before you became famous. Before you had a BMW and a house with a swimming pool. Not because I was jealous. I wasn't! You played a major role in *Second Coming*. You were the top gun. I suppose at one time I too looked upon you as a hero. A down and out heavy drinker who had beaten the odds and made it. But the truth is, for a good part of your life you were a drunk. I don't mean that as a putdown. I was a drunk too during most of those same years.

But having been an alcoholic myself, I know firsthand most drunks are not very nice people. Not you and not me. Not when we're drinking.

You wrote about life in a mean, lean way, but I can't help but think the poets who emulate your lifestyle must be lonely souls. There's nothing romantic about being a down and out writer. People who think there is are only fooling themselves.

What you represented was the American dream of making it; rising out of the slums and being able to spit in the face of the beast, even if the beast was sometimes yourself.

What you represented is individualism at its best, and at its worst; a crying appeal to a popular audience who could empathize. Look man, they can say, Bukowski made it, maybe there is hope for us too.

The important thing is that much of your writing showed empathy for the down and out; the damned and near-damned, and the not-yet-down-trodden souls of America. You threw out a lifeline to the drunks, the blue-collar workers and the assembly-line zombies barely able to make it home at night.

Your art rose high above the man himself. Your art was better than you were as a person, which only goes to show that in the end, the power of art prevails. And that, I believe, is what poetry is all about.

So there, I've said it. I love you Hank. That wasn't so hard. I'm only sad you found it so hard to say I love you to those people who reached out to you. That you had to put them down and shut them out of your life.

I hope the poem I wrote shortly after your death would meet with your approval:

Poem For All The Kids
Who Couldn't Get Enough Of Bukowski

These kids could never
Get enough of him
Not in books or magazines
Or on rare occasions in person
They wrote poems for and
About him
They bemoaned the fact that

He hadn't been accepted
By the academics
As if this were somehow
A liability
They flailed away
At the establishment
Supposedly on his behalf
But I suspect that
Getting their names in print
Had more than a little
To do with it

A few chastised him for
Not using semicolons
But were quick to forgive him
Because he was a genius
And a genius can do
Whatever he wants to do

To his credit
When fame discovered him
He quit writing hate poems
To those who had once
Befriended him
And if success did this
To him
Then she can't be half
The whore they make her out
To be

For a man who lived alone
For most of his life
He did remarkably well
And if he conned the small
Press editors and publishers
It was only because
He had the stamps to do it
And selling your soul

To the post office
All those years
Was no easy trip
Believe me I know
I've been there
And the readings never
Came easy for him
Puking his guts out
Behind stage
Or in some bar bathroom
Or on that one occasion
In San Francisco
On the side
Of Ferlinghetti's van
But fate was kind to him
It gave him Linda Lee and
A new lease on life and
A home in San Pedro and
How many years
She tacked on to his life
We'll never know

He would be the first
To tell you that
He was an asshole and
He was
And so are you and I
Sometimes more and
Sometimes less
Depending on
The circumstances

He would be the first
To admit that
He was a hustler and
A con man and
He was both
But he did it with style

The Holy Grail: Bukowski/Second Coming

Which is more
Than you can say
For most of us

What he wouldn't tell
All those young kids
Was what they wanted
To hear the most
That yes they were
Poets
That yes their work
Was dynamite
That they too could
Make it
If only they hung
In there
And flooded the littles
With their work
For the next
10 or 20 years
And the fates
Were kind to them
Failing that
There is always suicide
Or getting a job
At the post office

Amen
Rest in peace.

A Visionary . . .

A.D. Winans was born on January 12, 1936 in San Francisco, California where he has remained most all his life except for a tour of duty with the Air Force in Panama, where poverty-stricken streets sobered him on the condition of humanity outside the United States. In the late fifties he was swept up by the Beat consciousness and energy in the cafés and bars of San Francisco's North Beach. He heard Ginsberg and Ferlinghetti read for the first time and was emotionally moved, but it was Beat legend Bob Kaufman who helped shape A.D.'s lifestyle and literary career. Other influences included Kell Robertson (*Desperado*), Doug Blazek (*Ole*), poets William Wantling, Jack Micheline and, of course, Charles Bukowski.

Winans started Second Coming Press in 1972 and has remained a key figure in American literary life and the late twentieth century small press movement. He has written some thirty books (see back flap) as a poet and writer and published many books by others under his Second Coming imprint. Additionally, his literary magazine *Second Coming* published many well known and lesser known younger writers over the years.

A.D. Winans has also been involved in his local community with the San Francisco Arts Commission, Neighborhood Arts Program and the now defunct Federal CETA program; and with national literary organizations like COSMEP and the NEA, and in helping bring poetry into local schools and state prisons.